AF484148

NO BLACKS, NO WHITES: JUST THE HUMAN RACE

ISBN: 978-978-60880-4-4

Published in Nigeria by WORITAL GLOBAL, 2024
6b Lanre Awolokun Street, Gbagada Phase 2, Lagos, Nigeria.
WORITAL (hello@worital.com)
+2348114027024

Cover Design, Interior Layout, Print and Bound by:
WORITAL (hello@worital.com)

ACKNOWLEDGEMENT

This work is dedicated to my maker, Almighty God, who gave me the idea and resources to carry out this project. The completion of this book has also been made possible by my family, who are my support system, which includes my lovely wife, Ololade, and my incredible wiz-kids, Daniel and Samuel.

Special thanks to the fantastic team at Worital for making my ambition of proposing a solution to a global problem a reality.

A final dedication to the victims of genocide and ethnic cleansing. The global community would benefit from an increase in love rather than hate.

AUTHOR'S NOTE

What could be more dangerous than the brutal, inhumane realities of racism, prejudice, and discrimination inflicted upon innocent lives? These individuals are unjustly punished for "transgressions" rooted solely in their skin colour, nationality, or continent. Every facet of their existence—political, economic, social, and beyond—is profoundly marred by this disgusting phenomenon. It is agonising to acknowledge that discrimination, prejudice, and racism continue to etch deep scars on the lives of those targeted by racists. This scourge extends far beyond individuals residing in foreign lands, permeating even nations with diverse ethnic populations. It is a direct, relentless assault on the very essence of our shared humanity.

As a seasoned consultant abruptly terminated under the flimsy guise of being unqualified for a role I had excelled in for a decade in Nigeria, I came to viscerally understand that discrimination and racism are not mere blemishes on our society; they are insidious, corrosive forces capable of robbing people, even children, of their dreams and rendering life a hostile, unbearable ordeal. My heart shattered under the weight of the painful experiences I endured in my career. Yet, this very anguish ignited a burning desire within me to write a book aimed at awakening millions to the dire truth that racism and its insidious brethren pose a grave threat to every individual on this planet. They are ubiquitous, lurking in the shadows, ready to strike. I am unwavering in my conviction that racism, discrimination, and prejudice are the sworn enemies of humanity, inflicting untold suffering, crushing aspirations, and jeopardising the very existence of countless souls.

The harrowing incidents of racial abuse, tragically exemplified by the murder of George Floyd, which sent shockwaves of outrage across the globe, have ignited powerful movements like "Black Lives Matter" and countless other initiatives worldwide. My inspiration also flows from the poignant messages woven into the music of iconic artists like Michael Jackson ("Heal the World" & "Black or White") and Bob Marley ("War"), which boldly confront the scourges of racial injustice, discrimination, and tribalism. The time has come to staunch the flow of tears and end the unjust treatment inflicted upon individuals based on these abhorrent factors.

Love is the universal language, the most potent weapon to defeat this enemy. This book is my humble attempt to illuminate the path forward, to enlighten readers about the transformative power of compassion, empathy, and understanding as the tools we must wield to effect genuine, lasting change in our world. I envision a future where the spectre of racial discrimination is banished and where every individual is cherished and valued as an equal member of the human family. Ultimately, we are all human beings, each blessed with unique talents and potential, regardless of the hue of our skin or the place of our birth.

Let us not merely read these words but let them stir us to action. Let us embrace love as our guiding principle, and together, we can forge a world where justice, equality, and compassion reign supreme. The time for change is now, and the responsibility rests upon each of our shoulders. Let us rise to the challenge and build a brighter future for all.

CONTENTS

Chapter One

INTRODUCTION: A WORLD DIVIDED

"It is not our differences that divide us. We cannot recognise, accept, and celebrate those differences."
– Andre Lorde

Humans are humans, whether black, white or red. Humans were created in different forms, sizes and shapes to bring beauty to the world. However, we have been made to believe that some people are better than others, which has generated several cases of racism and tribalism that are scattered all over the world.

THE GLOBAL NATURE OF RACISM, TRIBALISM AND PREJUDICE:

According to Stephen Castles (1993), racism is a situation where certain social groups consider other groups inferior due to physical or cultural traits or national origin and use economic, social or political power to legitimise the exploitation or exclusion of the identified group. Similarly, Richard (2008) defines prejudice as a negative attitude towards an entire group, while discrimination is the behaviour that denies certain rights or opportunities to a group. This can be regarded as an attitude at the individual level that can either be positive or negative towards groups or their members. This attitude is responsible for creating and sustaining hierarchical status between groups.

It is crucial to mention that prejudice is a harmful phenomenon that is characterised by a strong aversion or dislike towards a group of people or an individual based on faulty and rigid generalisations. The Psychology of Prejudice defines it as a negative attitude which arises from preconceived notions about a person or group and is often unfounded or based on limited information. Prejudice can manifest in various forms, such as racism, sexism, homophobia, and religious intolerance, among others. It is a detrimental force that can lead to discrimination, oppression, and marginalisation of individuals or groups.

The global nature of racism, tribalism and prejudice can be traced to several social actions such as xenophobia, segregation, and others as commonly observed in every part of the world and systems where it is believed that racial equality does not exist.

The following are the factors responsible for the global nature of racism, tribalism and prejudice around the world:

1. The established economic structures aimed at perpetuating discrimination and inequality:

This is evident in the award of the course degree in the United States. According to the Report of the Committee on the Status of Minority Groups in the Economics Profession, PhDs in Economics were only awarded to Black economists. Black representation in the economic structure drastically reduced from 6 percent in 1995 to 3 percent in 2019. It was also reported that the Black representation in Economics was lower than in Science, Technology, Engineering and Mathematics.

Another critical effect of racism in the economic sector is employment discrimination. This occurs when qualified job applicants are denied employment by organisations based on gender, race or sex. In some cases, when you apply for jobs online and get an instant reply of "Unfortunately, you are not considered for the role," you can immediately suspect that an algorithm has been used to detect certain information in your profile, hence the negative response.

If it's not the case, why would employers ask for your nationality and your racial colour (such as White, Black, British, Non-British, White British, Black British, Hindu, Jew, Afro Caribbean, etc) before considering your suitability for a role? From my experience as a former job applicant, the information provided in such fields is a selection criterion for getting a job. This unfair and unjust treatment has deprived many qualified candidates from getting good jobs. It is expedient that this ill treatment from employers be stopped. Every qualified candidate for a role should be allowed to defend their qualifications, whether Black, White, British or Caucasian. There is a story of a female African-American job applicant in the US. She had applied for jobs severally but was always turned down. So, after applying for numerous jobs, all to no avail, she decided to experiment by changing her racial identification by selecting White American. Voila! She was invited for an interview. You can imagine the shock on the faces of her interviewers on seeing that she was not who they expected. It dawned on her that her ethnic profile had been responsible for her inability to get a job. What a shame. In some instances, some are underpaid and treated unjustly, leading to isolation and exclusion of the affected individual. This practice is not too far or unconnected with the illegal practice of modern slavery.

Consequently, the impact of economic discrimination can also cause a large wealth gap between the "favoured race" and the oppressed groups. This is also evident and common in many countries where certain people from stereotyped nations are denied house ownership or rent, especially when there are housing policies targeted at promoting unethical practices. The Jewish people also struggled with economic discrimination in the Middle Ages, majorly because of religious differences.

2. Colonialism and slavery targeted against other continents for global domination:

There are historical records of European countries that expanded their influences through the colonies established, particularly in Africa and Asia. This is evident in the policies of assimilation and association, of which the latter subjugated local administrations and imposed a foreign system of government on the affected countries. This also led to the introduction of new religions and cultures imposed on the people. That's why, to date, some Africans and citizens of countries that experienced slavery and/ or colonisation tend to feel inferior to the citizens of countries their colonisers hail from. Ending slavery and colonisation is just half the battle, emancipation of the minds of the people is a significant problem to tackle.

The transatlantic slave trade, which was one of the significant records of European colonialism, also caused the transportation of millions of Africans to Americans for hard labour. The psychological and emotional stress they were subjected to cannot be overlooked. They were also physically abused.

The preconceived mindset spread among people through the stereotypical news in the media:

A typical example is the negative news spread around by the media about the Northern parts of Nigeria. The Northern region of Nigeria has been painted with pictures of violence all over the internet, mainly creating false impressions about the Northerners as violent and bloody, particularly by those residing in the Southern part of the country.

In a viral video on Facebook, an American mentioned the unimaginable level of peace he enjoyed during his visit to Adamawa State, one of the states in Northern Nigeria, despite the exaggerated news about the level of insurgency in the country by international media outlets. This is not peculiar to Nigeria alone.

In a world where news spreads rapidly, many other countries can also be affected by media exaggerations. For instance, in Dubai, there is news about many Africans always being denied housing opportunities due to stereotypes about their countries. Many individuals will never have any business collaboration with those from other nations.

Political ideologies are also used to promote racist beliefs, especially in nations where certain "sets of people" are being denied opportunities to contest elections or hold political positions, depending on the system of government present in the country. A typical example is the Nazi ideology in Germany during the 1930s, which advocated the annihilation of "inferior" races such as Jews, Roma and Slaves, and the wrong conviction of the supremacy of the Aryan race. The Holocaust can also be traced to this ideology.

Inadequate education about the diversities of the human race largely contributes to this evil.

THE INTRODUCTION OF THE CONCEPT OF "NO BLACKS, NO WHITE; JUST HUMANS"

While reflecting on life, I was puzzled by the level of discrimination in the world where people are labelled and judged based on their skin colours and nationalities. This thought troubled me for some time, and it is imperative to state that it is disheartening and unsettling. While some are referred to as Caucasians, others are called Albinos and some individuals are referred to as Negroes, among other labels across the world.

It is essential to recognise that we all are humans, and it is wrong and inhumane to judge people based on their skin colour. Of course, this level of discrimination is a global phenomenon, which urgently calls for serious attention as there are reports of people who have been denied opportunities or privileges because of their nationalities or skin colour. There are shreds of evidence accompanying these unfortunate incidences, which have almost been institutionalised. Speaking of institutional racism, the British Met Police and a few other institutions are guilty of being institutionally racist. This is another dimension entirely. Unfortunately, there are cases of organisations or government departments favouring some people over others.

No one had the privilege to determine their skin colours or nationalities. We never had the opportunity to decide where we would have preferred to be our nations and continents; therefore, it is wrong to judge anyone for these. It is high time these cases stopped, as I firmly believe that no tribe should be considered inferior to another. Significantly, we must all outgrow that mentality and love one another as humans that we have always been.

THE PRIMARY GOALS OF THIS BOOK

This book is a clarion call for the complete eradication of all forms of discrimination, unconscious bias, tribalism, and ethnocentrism that plague our human interactions. It aspires to be a transformative force, shaping human behaviour towards one another, and a definitive reference text found in institutional libraries and personal bookshelves alike on the critical subjects of racism, discrimination, and tribalism. Its message is a resounding call to revive and nurture the innate humanism within each of us.

Recognising and Embracing Diversity:

A cornerstone of this book's message is recognising and understanding our inherent diversity as human beings. This is not merely a matter of tolerance but a profound appreciation of diversity's richness in our lives. Consider the analogy of a garden: a garden with only one type of flower may be visually appealing, but it lacks the vibrancy and multi-layered beauty of a garden bursting with diverse blooms. Similarly, a world populated by only one race would be monotonous and uninspiring.

This principle extends to the workplace. As an employer, imagine the immense satisfaction and creative potential unlocked when your workforce comprises individuals from diverse ethnic backgrounds. When these individuals interact and collaborate with tolerance and genuine understanding, innovation flourishes, and the workplace becomes a dynamic and fulfilling environment.

From Tolerance to Understanding:
Tolerance, while a necessary starting point, is not the ultimate goal. Tolerance implies enduring differences rather than embracing them. It is a passive stance that can easily give way to resentment or indifference. True progress is moving beyond tolerance and striving for deep, meaningful understanding. This means actively seeking to comprehend the unique perspectives, experiences, and cultural backgrounds of others. It means celebrating and maximising our differences rather than merely tolerating them.

The dangers of failing to move beyond tolerance are evident in the countless instances of violence, war, and hatred that have plagued human history. These conflicts are often fueled by ignorance, fear, and a lack of understanding of those different from us. By actively seeking understanding, we dismantle the foundations of these conflicts and pave the way for a more harmonious and peaceful world.

Love as the Antidote to Discrimination:

Love, in its purest form, is the most potent antidote to the poison of racial discrimination. It is the force that compels us to see the inherent worth and dignity in every human being, regardless of their race, ethnicity, or background. Love transcends the boundaries of difference and unites us in our shared humanity.

This message of diversity, tolerance, understanding, and love is not merely a philosophical ideal; it is a practical imperative. It is a message that must be urgently embraced by leaders, policymakers, and individuals alike if we are to effectively combat the scourge of racial discrimination and build a more just and equitable world.

The Beauty of Diversity:

Our world is a tapestry woven with threads of countless colours, each representing a unique race, ethnicity, or culture. This diversity is not a source of division but a wellspring of creativity, innovation, and resilience. It is what makes our world a vibrant and fascinating place.

Consider the richness of human expression found in the diverse languages, music, art, and cuisine of our planet. Each of these is a testament to the unique contributions of different cultures and a reminder that our differences are not something to be feared but to be celebrated.

In science and technology, diversity of thought and experience has led to groundbreaking discoveries and innovations. When individuals from different backgrounds come together to solve problems, they bring a more comprehensive range of perspectives and approaches, leading to more creative and effective solutions.

Even in the natural world, diversity is essential for the health and resilience of ecosystems. A diverse ecosystem is better equipped to adapt to changing conditions and withstand environmental pressures. This principle applies equally to human societies. A diverse culture is more robust, more resilient, and more adaptable.

The primary goals of this book are not merely to inform but to inspire action. It seeks to empower readers with the knowledge, tools, and motivation to become agents of change in their own lives and communities. By embracing diversity, fostering understanding, and cultivating love, we can overcome the divisive forces of racism, discrimination, and tribalism and build a world where all individuals are valued, respected, and empowered to reach their full potential.

12

Chapter Two

A HISTORICAL PERSPECTIVE

"I am not concerned with your liking or disliking me.
All I ask is that you respect me as a human being."
– Jackie Robinson

THE ROOTS OF RACISM AND DISCRIMINATION THROUGHOUT HISTORY

Unfortunately, the roots of racism, tribalism, ethnocentricity and all forms of discrimination are not unconnected with slavery and its effects. In the ancient Greek empire, there was a widespread belief that some people were born to be superior to others due to historical practices. This wrong notion means that these "superior" people have to take leadership positions for others to follow and suffer discriminatory practices. There is also a belief that the gods are responsible for the appointment of certain people to the elite positions of leadership over the "unfortunate" people. Erroneously, the Greeks believe that leadership is reserved for the few chosen by a direct power to control, manage and direct the lives, futures and aspirations of the unchosen. The idea of superiority is still in existence as many still uphold their conservative discriminatory mindsets.

The saddening prosecution of the Jews, mainly based on religion, can also be traced to the Middle Ages and anti-Semitism in Europe. During this period, Jewish people were subjected to economic discrimination and higher taxes. They were denied the opportunity to be moneylenders as they were also accused of causing widespread diseases. These untrue allegations caused explosions from European countries on innocent lives. Fanatics also claimed that they were responsible for the death of Jesus. (Princeton University, 2018)

With the above explanations, it is impossible to disconnect racism from the slavery practices introduced by European powers. During that era, enslaved people were not treated as human beings. They were regarded as "inferior." Several books consulted on this topic also record that many leaders were appointed based on their bodily features, such as pointed noses and fair skin. The leaders were often regarded as the "civilised" ones. In European countries, many white men were chosen for leadership positions in government and business.

THE TRANS-ATLANTIC SLAVE TRADE, APARTHEID IN SOUTH AFRICA AND THE HOLOCAUST

According to Nunn (2008), the history of Africa is closely tied to slavery, as it has undergone four major slave trades. These include the trans-Saharan, Red Sea, and Indian Ocean slave trades, all dating back to at least 800 AD. Research shows that the regions of Africa from which the largest number of enslaved people were taken between 1400 and 1900 are now part of the poorest regions on the continent.

Koigi (2024) argues that the robbery of African nations through the forced removal of men and women in their prime to Western countries not only resulted in economic loss for the continent but also contributed to the high level of poverty that exists today. More than 12 million men and women were forcibly taken from their native lands as enslaved people in America and Europe.

THE TRANS-ATLANTIC SLAVE TRADE

The Trans-Atlantic Slave Trade is considered one of the most tragic experiences in the world, spurred by the demand for labour in European colonies. The Editors of Encyclopaedia noted that it profoundly impacted the African continent, leaving it destabilised and vulnerable to conquest for centuries. Reports also indicated that nearly two million people died due to starvation and disease during the brutal Middle Passage across the ocean. About 10 to 12 million enslaved Black Africans were transported across the Atlantic Ocean to America from the 16th to the 19th century.

The slave traders subjected the captives to all forms of emotional, mental and physical abuse. This is common to the gory cases of enslaved person trades all over the world, as discussed in other areas of life. The survivors of the trade were sold to the Americans and subjected to hard labour for plantations and mines. The positive impact of the trade on the European economy cannot be undervalued, especially in manufacturing and banking, as it created an avenue for financial domination and wealth generation. It is also pertinent to emphasise that the level of systemic racism can be traced to the trade.

APARTHEID

According to the Oxford Advanced Learner's Dictionary, apartheid is defined as a policy of racial discrimination and segregation, particularly one that favours minority rule. Historically, apartheid was the campaign slogan for the White-led Nationalist Party in 1948 until the emergence of F.W De Klerk as President in 1989. His assumption of office led to the eradication of the institutionalised system. The enforcement of apartheid was passed into law, which caused a complete separation between racial groups at every stage in life.

Azi (2023) reveals that the concept of apartheid was introduced in South Africa through the pro-Afrikaner party, the National

Party (NP), as part of their strategies to protect the country's economic and social system with white domination and racial domination. In his article in the International Journal of Science and Society, the "Big Apartheid" was introduced in the 1960s to oppress blacks through police tyranny and territorial alienation. This continued until Nelson Mandela's resolution in his struggle against the apartheid regime, which led to his arrest in 1964 and eventual 18-year imprisonment on Robben Island. Despite his incarceration, he was persistent and resilient in the face of daunting, overwhelming encumbrances.

THE HOLOCAUST

Following the Nazi regime during World War II, the holocaust is identified as the tragic genocide of approximately six million Europeans, Jews and other minority groups. The promotion of extreme nationalism and anti-semitism is connected to the emergence of Adolf Hitler and his party, the Nazi Party, in the 1930s. It was reported that the Jews were subjected to poor living conditions and abject poverty. Some of them also battled forced labour and emotional and mental health challenges. There were camps primarily established to murder and torture the affected individuals.

THE IMPACT OF COLONIALISM ON RACIAL TENSION

One of the lasting impacts of colonialism is the false belief that "foreigners" are superior to anyone, as observed particularly among many Nigerians, mainly due to their white skin. It is high time we let go of the impression of superiority imposed through colonialism and other inhumane treatments and stepped into the realities of the present age. No one is inferior to another.

Slavery has long been abolished, but the battle has gone to the mind. It is regarded as a psychological stronghold that has bound people; many individuals have not recovered. This scenario perfectly explains this point: If you tie a horse to a peg and leave it there for a long time, by the time you remove the rope, the horse will still believe that it is still pegged to that spot and feel that it is beyond its power to move from there. This is referred to as mental slavery. It has gone beyond binding with physical chains and transitioned to the mindset of people, chaining them and restricting them from becoming the best versions of themselves. This can be described as the "Invincible peg syndrome."

According to the United Nations Human Rights (2023), the impact of colonialism on racial tension is intricately linked with racism, racial discrimination, xenophobia, and intolerance faced by Africans, people of African descent, people of Asian descent, and indigenous people. Verene Shepherd, the Chair of the Committee on the Elimination of Racial Discrimination, presented a report to the 54th session of the Human Rights Council highlighting environmental degradation, economic underdevelopment, racial profiling, systemic racism, and poor infrastructure in the education and health sectors as the effects of colonialism. They include unequal access to healthcare and social injustice, stating that expected development following independence never materialised for many former colonial countries.

In some former colonies, ethnic rivalry is also a negative impact of colonialism. Sandra Marker (2003) links the conflict between Greek and Turkish Cypriots to British colonial rule, where both populations were merged as a means of control. When Greek Cypriots opposed the merger, the British encouraged Turkish Cypriots to oppose them, leading to ethnic conflict and deep division between the two populations after the British departed. Violence encouraged during British rule continued erupting periodically. Collete (2015) also shows that British tactics of "divide and rule" caused divisions between the Buganda kingdom and the rest of Uganda. This resulted in inequalities in education, economy, and infrastructure between the South and the North due to neoliberal racism. Furthermore, it motivated Ugandans to ethnically discriminate against their people in aid of economic sustainability and development.

Malesela (2021) asserts that colonialism fostered racial discrimination to perpetuate separation in a continent whose kingdoms were founded on peace and unity. The magnitude of racial alienation still influences and marginalises Africans even in the post-colonial era.

The US colonial practices on FilAm (Filipinx/a/o/Americans) migration can also be linked to structural racism, which is defined as the methods by which laws, policies, institutions, and social norms are enacted to legalise and perpetuate White dominance and supremacy. This results in Asian Americans' invisibility in healthcare services and resource allocation decisions despite experiencing high rates of hypertension, breast and prostate cancer, and type 2 diabetes and having limited access to mental health services compared to White Americans (Melanie et al., 2022).

THE LINGERING SHADOW OF SLAVERY: HISTORICAL ROOTS OF CONTEMPORARY ISSUES

The spectre of slavery continues to haunt our world, casting a long and ominous shadow over contemporary issues, particularly in the realms of social inequality, racism, and discrimination. Its insidious influence permeates various sectors, including economics, health, labour, and beyond, perpetuating cycles of disadvantage and injustice.

The false narrative of slavery, which projected an image of inherent inferiority onto those who were enslaved, has left a lasting legacy of dehumanisation. Many individuals, mainly those descended from enslaved populations, continue to face systemic barriers that limit their opportunities and perpetuate their marginalisation. They are often relegated to substandard living conditions, treated as second-class citizens, and denied access to the same resources and privileges enjoyed by others.

The insidiousness of this historical legacy lies in the fact that it has ingrained a deep-seated belief in the superiority of certain groups over others. This belief manifests in a range of attitudes and behaviours, from overt acts of racism to more subtle forms of discrimination. It fuels a toxic narrative that perpetuates social hierarchies and justifies the unequal treatment of individuals based on their race or ethnicity.

The persistence of this mindset is evident in the words and actions of those who cling to outdated notions of racial superiority. They may harbour a belief that their ancestors' status as slaveholders entitles them to continued dominance over those they perceive as their inferiors. This distorted view of history fuels a sense of entitlement and perpetuates a cycle of prejudice and discrimination.

The consequences of this historical legacy are far-reaching and devastating. They manifest in the economic disparities that exist between different racial and ethnic groups, in the health inequities that disproportionately affect marginalised communities, and in the workplace discrimination that limits opportunities for advancement.

To overcome this legacy, we must confront the historical roots of racism and discrimination. This requires acknowledging the profound harm caused by slavery and its enduring impact on contemporary society. It also necessitates a commitment to dismantling the systems and structures that perpetuate inequality and injustice.

THE SCARS OF COLONIALISM: FUELING RACIAL TENSIONS

Colonialism, a dark chapter in human history, has left deep scars that continue to plague and fuel racial tensions in the present day. The narrative of white supremacy, which was used to justify the colonisation and exploitation of vast regions of the world, has had a lasting impact on the global psyche.

This narrative has created a sense of inferiority among many individuals subjected to its insidious influence. It has led to internalised racism, where individuals internalise the negative stereotypes and prejudices directed at their group, leading to low self-esteem, psychological trauma, and a range of other mental and emotional health issues.

The legacy of colonialism is also evident in the political landscape. Many groups that were marginalised and disenfranchised during the colonial era continue to struggle for representation and power in the political arena. This lack of representation perpetuates a cycle of marginalisation and reinforces existing power imbalances.

The historical record of violence and cultural erasure that occurred during the colonial era also contributes to racial tensions in the present day. The forced assimilation of Indigenous populations, the suppression of their languages and cultures, and the violent displacement of communities have left lasting scars that continue to affect intergroup relations.

Addressing the legacy of colonialism requires a multi-faceted approach. It involves acknowledging the historical injustices perpetrated during the colonial era and taking concrete steps to rectify them. This may include initiatives aimed at promoting cultural revitalisation, supporting indigenous self-determination, and addressing the economic and social disparities that have arisen as a result of colonialism.

It also requires challenging the narrative of white supremacy that continues to permeate many aspects of our society. This involves promoting a more inclusive and equitable understanding of history, one that recognises the contributions and perspectives of all groups, regardless of their race or ethnicity.

By confronting the historical roots of racism and discrimination, we can begin to heal the wounds of the past and build a more just and equitable future for all. This is a complex and challenging task, but it is essential for the well-being of our global community.

Chapter Three

UNDERSTANDING RACISM, DISCRIMINATION AND TRIBALISM

"There is no such thing as race. None. There is just a human race —scientifically, anthropologically."
- Toni Morrison.

Racism, Tribalism, Discrimination and the like cannot be adequately understood without a clear definition of the terms. The need to conceptualise these words gave rise to different attempts by scholars to define the concepts. In this chapter, we will examine a few of the definitions of these concepts for a better understanding of the concepts.

THE DEFINITION OF RACISM, PREJUDICE, DISCRIMINATION, TRIBALISM, ETHNOCENTRISM, AND UNCONSCIOUS BIAS

RACISM

Racism is defined as the act of promoting division. It promotes the concept of "you are not from here." This is one of the best definitions of racism that is so relatable. According to the Oxford Advanced Learner's Dictionary, racism is the "belief that there are distinct human races which are inherently different, such that a person's abilities are determined by their race, and generally that some races are superior and others inferior."

Grosfoguel (2011) defines racism as a global system of hierarchy that establishes superiority and inferiority among human races. This system has been established politically, economically and culturally for centuries by the institutions of the capitalist/patriarchal, western-centric, Christian-centric, modern/colonial world. Bowseer (2017) noted that the word "racism" gained popularity in the United States during the 20th century to describe social conflicts and is used interchangeably with the term "racial discrimination." Additionally, Cape (2022) defines racism as a definitive psychological process through which individuals are categorised, which leads to discrimination.

PREJUDICE

The Cambridge Dictionary explains "prejudice" as an unjust opinion or feeling formed without one's knowledge. This occurs when people are profiled and judged harshly by concluding people from a certain place behave the same way. For example, if a person is loud, he may get questions like "Are you from Nigeria because all Nigerians are loud?" Such a question is a typical example of prejudice. Another example of prejudice is when someone makes a general statement like "all men are cheats" because they have dated men who cheated on them or claimed that "all women are liars" when a lady breaks your heart. Some people may be prejudicial towards Nigerians because of what happened to Hushpuppy during his fraud case. They may conclude that all Nigerians are fraudsters. But that's wrong. Every tribe has a mix of good and bad people. Therefore, every tribe has its fair share of good and bad people.

There is no tribe that is entirely good or entirely bad. On a lighter note, this consciousness of being susceptible to prejudice as a Nigerian (because of an image in dire need of repair) almost made me reject and react when a hotel receptionist handed me the key card to room 419. I wasn't sure whether to laugh or be angry. Lots of questions were raging in my mind, such as "Is this intentional because the hotel management figured I'm a Nigerian and they've heard about numerous cases of scammers and fraudsters (aka 419ers) who are Nigerians? Call it my own "battlefield of the mind." I had to snap out of it and resolve to enjoy my stay and focus on the training I came to deliver in that location.

DISCRIMINATION

Discrimination can be defined simply as the unfair treatment of a person or a group of people because of their gender, skin colour or tribe. It can manifest in various forms, like hate speeches and biases in the workplace. According to the American Psychological Association, discrimination is defined as the "unfair or prejudicial treatment of people based on characteristics such as race, gender, age or sexual orientation."

Historically, discrimination has been institutionalised through laws and policies, such as racial segregation in the US and apartheid in South Africa. Despite legal protections, discriminatory practices still exist in contemporary times. For instance, there are cases of barriers to education for some marginalised groups, and racial profiling and gender pay gaps are still prevalent in the world.

ETHNOCENTRISM

Anthony (2022) defines ethnocentrism as an attitude that leads to judging other cultures as inferior to one's own, which can result in stereotyping, discrimination, and xenophobia. Bizumi (2015) defines ethnocentrism as a belief that one's cultural or ethnic group is superior to others, often leading to negative attitudes towards those outside the group. Sociologists and anthropologists introduced this term, which has since become an interdisciplinary concept. Ethnocentrism is usually associated with racism, discrimination, and prejudice. According to The African Diaspora and the Development of American Culture (2022), ethnocentrism is negatively judging other cultures while using one's culture as the standard, which creates division. This belief can lead to the perception that one's culture is superior to others.

TRIBALISM

Tribalism, according to the Merriam-Webster dictionary, is the state of being organised into a tribe or tribes. Abdelrahim (2022) interprets tribalism as an unethical practice deemed reasonable for the connection of kith and kin in their tribes towards their access to resources. The Encyclopaedia of World Geography provides another definition of tribalism as the identification with a particular ethnic group or tribe, which appears paradoxical to nationalism, which is the devotion to the interests and culture of one's society. While it's okay to love your tribe, of course, it's your right to, and it's your heritage, moderation or caution is needed so as not to allow ourselves to become tribalistic. I know people who don't believe in marriage outside of their tribe and have resolved to influence who their children will marry, making sure they keep it within their tribe. This can be a form of being close-minded and not open to other ways of life. This can play out even in the workplace, where tribe is placed before competence.

UNCONSCIOUS BIAS

Unconscious bias refers to a form of judgment that results from subtle cognitive processes that operate outside of regular thought processes and control. It is rooted in the formation of conclusions about individuals and situations influenced by personal background, experiences, memories, and cultural environment. In her presentation on Managing Unconscious Bias, Jonnelle succinctly defines unconscious bias as an unintentional, subtle, and subconscious decision that can happen to anyone. Similarly, Firth, in his guidance on recruitment panel issues for the Scottish Government, characterises unconscious bias as a process whereby judgements and decisions are based on prior experiences, assumptions, and interpretations we may be unaware of. Shine Professional Chartered Psychologists explain unconscious bias as our unintentional people preferences, which enable us to engage people without making quick decisions. Research demonstrates that unconscious bias operates in less than a tenth of a second, making it faster than the speed at which our eyes can process an image.

EXPLORING DIFFERENT TYPES OF RACISM (SYSTEMIC, INSTITUTIONAL, INDIVIDUAL)

INSTITUTIONAL RACISM: This term refers to the policies, practices, and procedures of an organisation which result in the preferential treatment of particular individuals of the same colour while simultaneously causing harm to individuals of other colours. This form of discrimination, as defined by the Alberta Civil Liberties Research Centre, stems from the actions of individuals who are prejudiced or exist within a discriminatory society.

Encyclopaedia Britannica editors additionally define institutional racism as discrimination that is predominantly based on race by political, economic, and legal systems. Notably, the Out of Africa Monologue series defines the term as a set of racial attitudes prevalent in an ethnic group's traditions, beliefs, opinions, and myths, as well as in their practices. Such attitudes may persist over extended periods in a manner that normalises demonising the human worth of others. There have been recent reports in the news about some public institutions in the United Kingdom found to be institutionally racist. A straightforward test to confirm the presence of institutional racism could be sieving through an organisation's past and current leadership structure (especially if they're multinational or operate in a multicultural society) to see how diverse it has been. That's one of the things I try to check before aspiring to work in an organisation, so I'm sure there's no glass ceiling for people of my type to rise to the highest possible rank.

SYSTEMIC RACE: The Canadian Race Relations Foundation defines systemic racism as a complex and interconnected relationship between individual, institutional, and structural levels, which work together as a system of racism. The various levels of racism operate in a coordinated manner and function together as a system of racism. Braveman et al. (2022) also define systemic racism as the involvement of entire systems (legal, political, healthcare, and others), often perpetuating unfair treatment of people of colour.

According to the Anti-Racism Education Toolkit, systemic racism is a form of racism that is embedded within the structures of a society rather than being the result of individual actions. An example of this can be seen in the Australian government, which was established during the colonial period. The legal, political, and economic systems that were put in place at that time were designed to favour the Western culture and values, which has resulted in a systemic disadvantage for other cultures and communities.

Sebastiaan (2020) suggests the need to break down racism, which is still present in South Africa due to the deliberate actions of individuals and systems. We must strive to become a bridge that genuinely connects with others as we contribute to each other's humanity.

INDIVIDUAL RACISM: According to Law Insider, individual racism is a term used to describe prejudicial behaviour, bias or discrimination by an individual based on their race, skin colour, national origin, or ethnicity. This form of racism may be either intentional or unintentional, and it can manifest in various ways, such as making a racist joke, believing in the superiority of white people, or crossing the street to avoid passing a Black man (Fitchburg State University).

HOW DISCRIMINATION MANIFESTS IN VARIOUS ASPECTS OF LIFE

According to a viral video on Twitter, Irish people never faced the same discrimination as Black people who suffered under chattel slavery. However, they were not at the top of society either. They were enslaved similarly to Africans, although they did not have to endure forced labour solely because they were Irish. In 1662, a law in the Virginia colonies called "partus sequitur ventrum" stated that if a woman was enslaved and African, her children would also be enslaved based on their race. Irish people in the United States were subjected to indentured servitude, a system of forced labour where individuals had contracts or were forced to pay off debts, which was different from chattel slavery.

Both indentured servitude and chattel slavery were outlawed in 1865 under the 13th Amendment, except as punishment. Irish people in the United States faced discrimination based on ethnicity, class, religion, and xenophobia. They were eventually assimilated and viewed as White, which was an exciting transformation.

Race is a human construct created to differentiate and separate people. While we naturally have differences in skin tone, facial features, and hair texture, race encompasses the politics and meanings associated with these physical traits. Dorothy Roberts describes race as a political category disguised as a biological one, where people are racialised based on societal and political needs.

Starting in the 1840s, Irish people were subjected to racialisation and stereotypes similar to Black people. Irish immigrants in the US were allowed to marry other White people but did not have the same privileges and rights. Since 1878, US courts have debated whether certain groups are considered Whites. Unfortunately, early Irish immigrants in the US contributed to the oppression of Black Americans, demonstrating harsh treatment towards them. Irish immigrants in New York and Boston even controlled the police force, further perpetuating white supremacy.

Irish American history illustrates how the concept of whiteness can be inconsistent. While Irish people are now considered white, not everyone in Ireland is white. A person's perceived whiteness often depends on their support of white supremacy.

MEDAL CEREMONY IN DUBLIN:
Footage also emerged showing a black young gymnast appearing to be snubbed during a medal ceremony in Dublin in March 2022. This also reveals the level of racial discrimination in sports. Four-

time Olympic champion Simone Biles says that "the incident broke my heart." The girl's mother said she believes Gymnastics Ireland has failed to apologise publicly. The body said, "The official in question had not been accepted but stressed that it had not been intentional." They said that after the complaint, a "resolution" had been agreed by both parties in August 2023.

CHINESE SUPERMARKET

Have you ever imagined a people discriminated against in their own country? What would have been their fate if they were in a racist country? According to a report by First Post America, a Chinese supermarket in Africa has allegedly been denying Nigerians entry, sparking controversy and accusations of racism. The incident occurred in Abuja, where residents were outraged after the supermarket was caught in the act. The video of the incident went viral, prompting the Federal Competition and Consumer Protection Commission (FCCPC) to shut down the supermarket until further notice.

As at the time the video was transcribed, it is unclear how the issue of Chinese racism against Nigerians surfaced, but it is reported that a group of Nigerians went to the supermarket to shop and were stopped by guards who only allowed people of Chinese descent to enter. In total condemnation of the act, the Nigerian authorities have refused to reopen the supermarket.

Reports also suggest that Chinese social media is filled with anti-black racist content, according to watchdog groups. This is not the first instance of Chinese racism, as it has been highlighted even before the COVID-19 pandemic.

TRIBALISM AMONG NIGERIANS

Following the defeat of the Igbo tribe in their attempt to secede from Nigeria in 1967 during the leadership of Odumegwu Ojukwu, there has been a deep resentment towards the Igbo culture as this is prevalent in the political space. In his article titled "A History of Ethnic Tension and Resentment," Chinua Achebe laments the resentment towards the Igbo tribe among other ethnic groups in Nigeria. According to his submission, this was fuelled by the introduction of the Federal Character principle, which aimed to address the perceived dominance of the Igbo tribe in education and civil service. Achebe also cites the forceful removal of Professor Eni Njoku as the Vice Chancellor of the University of Lagos as an example of the discrimination faced by the Igbo tribe. Professor Kenneth Onwuka Dike, the then Vice Chancellor of the University of Ibadan, also suffered a similar fate.

Obasanjo's Reaction to Igbophobia:

In a news report on Linda Ikeji's blog dated March 25, 2023, former President Olusegun Obasanjo was reported to have condemned the aversion of Nigerians to the Igbos. He mentioned that this aversion was responsible for the adverse reactions he received from many Nigerians after the appointment of Professor

Chukwuma Soludo and Ngozi Okonjo-Iweala as CBN governor and Finance minister, respectively, during his administration.

He also stated that the appointments of these two individuals in his government were probably some of the best appointments he made during his administration due to their outstanding achievements for the growth and development of the country. It is worth imagining how tribalism would have affected the country's progress if President Olusegun Obasanjo was not detribalised.

HOLIDAY IN ATHENS

Have you ever walked into a place full of strangers, and you can feel it on your skin that eyes are prying on you? You may even begin to feel like the next question they will ask is, "Excuse me, are you lost?" or "From which planet did you drop?" To make matters worse, they are not even speaking your language. That was how I felt my first time holidaying in Athens, Greece. I must commend the Greeks, as their hospitality and kindness is astounding. Everyone I interacted with made it a duty to advise me on safety and security. I was even advised to be more careful with my gadgets, especially my phone, since I was going about with it.

My interpretation of their look and behaviour is, "Look, dude! We're on the same level and not too different, skin colour aside!" Interestingly, I got a completely different reaction in the UK on my first visit. There, people stared at you with so much disgust and rudeness. I may be wrong (and right) with my judgement of people's attitudes in the UK; however, the point remains that attitude can be felt. No one is a perfect judge of character.

This racial attitude is further depicted in the way you're spoken to. I never once experienced anyone in Greece looking disgusted or disappointed when they realised I couldn't speak Greek. Many were kind enough to attempt to engage with me in English, which I found very hospitable because, without it, my holiday would have been downright horrible. In some countries, the inability to speak their language can be greeted with so much irritation; they would almost make you feel as if you were committing an abominable act.

While some countries like the UK are leading the DEI (Diversity, Equity and Inclusivity) drive, many are still light years behind and need to catch up. Even if having a BAME (Black Asian & Minority Ethnic Groups) in your organisation is like playing to the gallery, it should be commended. The only problem is when the entire cast of a contemporary movie only features someone of a different skin type, making it evident that it is a tick-box exercise. My dad refers to that when he says, "I'm praying and fasting because you told me to, not because I want to."

Until people know the essence of DEI, it will continue to be a tick-box exercise or even ignored entirely. Its purpose is to create a fair and equitable world where variety is made to thrive. Our differences should be strengths, not weaknesses. It should be regarded as an opportunity, not a threat.

Would you choose the unknown over the known because most people won't? That's why we tend to only relate with people we are familiar with or prefer to do business with. It is easy to fall into that trap of only wanting to do business with someone who speaks our language or looks like us (skin type). While it is not entirely wrong to go from the known to the unknown, we need to try to grow past these types of sentiments. The world needs variety. Look at any forest. It is made up of diverse species of plants and animals. That is how the ecosystem, which we are also part of, thrives.

POSSIBLE SIGNS THAT SHOW YOU ARE A RACIST (OR TEND TO BE ONE)

- You feel irritated by others speaking a language different to yours, and you do not understand what they're saying. The critical point is getting angry at others for speaking their languages is one of the highest forms of racism. Since we must embrace our diversity, it is pertinent to feel OK when others express themselves in a comfortable language. Additionally, feeling that your language is superior to other languages should not be encouraged.

- You criticise the prejudiced harshly due to your misconceived mindset of them and display a condescending attitude. This could also occur in workplaces, in the disciplinary committee, and other places, even in governmental positions where racism is institutionalised. In the judiciary system in countries where racism has almost been institutionalised, stiffer punishments are likely given to the affected individuals.

- You falsely disqualify the person's or group's intelligence, cultural level, social status or other merits, even in the face of apparent qualities.

- You always have exaggerated reactions to the misconduct of those battling racism. When people struggling with racism commit any offences, they tend to face exaggerated reactions from their bosses or colleagues who are racists.

- You oppress people based on their skin colour. You begin to form instant judgements or opinions about people of specific skin colour at first sight. Unfortunately, some people have issues with other people because of their appearance. Why should anyone be judged harshly for what you never had control over?

- You have the presumption that all members of your race should be racists, also. You don't like to see them relate with other people of different races, just like you do. Unrepentant racists always assume that everyone around them should also join them in their discrimination. They tend to have problems with those who decide to show humane treatment towards others.

- You are most likely to sit elsewhere or stand rather than sit with someone obviously from a different tribe (maybe by how they dress or look).

This is not an exhaustive list but an attempt to foster further discussion around the subject.

Chapter Four

XENOPHOBIA

"I see what is possible when we recognise that we are one American family, all deserving of equal treatment."
– Barack Obama

It can be defined as an act of violence towards a person or persons of a different ethnic group based on fear of domination. It is derived from the Greek words "Xenos," meaning "stranger" or "foreigner," and "Phobos," meaning "fear." It is a pervasive phenomenon ingrained in societies worldwide. It manifests as an irrational fear, suspicion, or hatred of those perceived as outsiders, often leading to discrimination, violence, and societal division.

This chapter aims to delve into the multifaceted nature of xenophobia, examining its causes, consequences, and notable cases across the globe.

UNDERSTANDING XENOPHOBIA:

Xenophobia is not a novel concept. Its roots can be traced back centuries, driven by economic competition, cultural differences, and political tensions. In contemporary society, globalisation has intensified interactions between diverse cultures, triggering fears of cultural dilution or economic displacement among certain groups. Additionally, political rhetoric and media sensationalism often exploit xenophobic sentiments for ideological or electoral gains, exacerbating social tensions.

CAUSES OF XENOPHOBIA:

1. **Economic Insecurity:** In times of economic instability, individuals may scapegoat immigrants or minority groups for job losses or financial hardships, perpetuating the belief that they are threats to native livelihoods.

2. **Cultural Clash:** Differences in language, religion, and customs can fuel distrust and hatred towards outsiders, fostering a sense of cultural superiority and the marginalisation of minority communities.

3. **Nationalism and Identity Politics:** Politicians and extremist groups may exploit nationalist ideologies to promote exclusionary policies and vilify immigrants as "others" who threaten national identity and security.

4. **Media Influence:** The way the media portrays immigrants and foreign groups can shape the perception of the citizens of

the host country. Negative portrayals or coverage can reinforce stereotypes, thereby causing xenophobic attitudes.

5. **Greed**: Sometimes, resources are not scarce; they are just highly valuable. A gold rush on Cherokee land in 1829 was one of the reasons the U.S. government displaced Native Americans from their lands during the Trail of Tears.

6. **History**: Past conflicts between different ethnic groups can leave lasting scars, thereby causing conflicting parties to develop distrust and hatred towards themselves.

CONSEQUENCES OF XENOPHOBIA:

1. **Social Division**: Xenophobia creates rifts within societies, undermining social cohesion and fostering mistrust between different ethnic or cultural groups.

2. **Human Rights Violations**: Discriminatory policies, hate crimes, and xenophobic rhetoric contribute to the violation of human rights, perpetuating cycles of inequality and injustice.

3. **Economic Impacts**: Xenophobic attitudes can hinder economic growth by deterring foreign investment, limiting labour mobility, and fostering a hostile environment for cultural exchange and innovation.

4. **Psychological and Physical Impacts:** Individuals who are targets of xenophobia often go through fear, anxiety, stress, etc. This can leave them with long-term mental health consequences.

Additionally, xenophobia can lead to physical violence and even loss of lives, which can cause immediate and devastating harm to victims.

5. **Global Consequences:** Xenophobia can strain diplomatic ties between countries, especially if one nation feels its citizens are unfairly treated abroad.

NOTABLE CASES OF XENOPHOBIA:

1. **United States**: The resurgence of nativist rhetoric and anti-immigrant policies, exemplified by the Trump administration's "Muslim ban" and family separation policies, fuelled xenophobic sentiments and exacerbated racial tensions.

2. **European Union:** The refugee crisis sparked a wave of xenophobia across Europe, with countries like Hungary and Poland adopting stringent immigration policies and far-right parties gaining traction on anti-immigrant platforms.

3. **South Africa**: Xenophobic attacks targeting African immigrants, mainly from Zimbabwe, Nigeria, and Somalia, have plagued South Africa for years, fuelled by economic competition and social resentment.

4. **Myanmar:** The persecution of the Rohingya Muslim minority by the Myanmar military, accompanied by widespread

discrimination and violence, reflects entrenched xenophobic attitudes towards ethnic and religious minorities.

5. **India:** The Citizenship Amendment Act (CAA) and National Register of Citizens (NRC) sparked protests and international condemnation for discriminating against Muslim immigrants and undermining secular principles, fuelling xenophobic tensions.

6. **Northern Nigeria versus Southern Nigeria (and vice versa):** There was a time when the North feared that the South, especially South Easterners, might become very powerful and dominate the rest of the country, hence the need to clip their wings. A prominent Northern leader, Sir Ahmadu Bello (the Sardauna of Sokoto), confirmed this in an interview he had with a foreign media in 1961 (See: https://youtu.be/5_odAy4rVz8?si=8XsBx5gp_egruxC-).

This is what led to the "pogrom" (a term used by the British to describe the wanton killing of people and destruction of properties in Eastern Nigeria) during the Civil War. Some viewed it not as war but more as ethnic cleansing, similar to what played out in Rwanda and Israel.

Fast forward to the early 2000s, and the reverse is now the case. Those fighting for their relevance in the country are now the Northern Nigeria, especially the Fulani tribe. Videos surfaced online where some Fulani herdsmen claimed Nigeria hates them and doesn't want them to exist by restricting cattle rearing through nomadic means, hence their need to fight back.

As long as we have the mindset of "this is my land, it doesn't belong to you, go to your land or go back to yours, go elsewhere but not just here," then there'll likely be cases of Xenophobia. That's why I wasn't comfortable with Donald Trump's slogan of "America first" during the campaign leading to his election victory as President of the United States because it had every colouration of the "Northernisation agenda" promoted by Sir Ahmadu Bello. It doesn't always lead to a good place. No wonder acts of ethnic-related crimes, such as George Floyd's case, happened during Donald Trump's reign. Leaders should never underestimate their influence. People can interpret what they say, didn't say, how they looked or failed to look, or their slightest action to mean a thing and act based on it, so they must be cautious.

Xenophobia remains a formidable challenge in an increasingly interconnected world, perpetuating discrimination, violence, and social division. Addressing xenophobia requires a concerted effort to promote empathy, tolerance, and inclusivity, challenging discriminatory attitudes and policies at the individual, societal, and institutional levels. By fostering a culture of acceptance and respect for diversity, we can mitigate the destructive impact of xenophobia and build a more equitable and harmonious global community.

Chapter Five

THE ROLE OF MEDIA IN PERPETUATING RACISM

"**I** thought I had received a death sentence in Nasarawa after reading my call-up letter on the National Youth Service Corps' portal, requesting my relocation to the state in the North Central of Nigeria, "Samuel said. He continued, "My eyes were filled with tears. My mind raced heavily throughout the night while reflecting on the slim chance of surviving in the so-called deadly geopolitical zone."

Narrating his sad experience after checking the dashboard, he further said, "My heart was shattered and broken into pieces like someone who just lost his loved one. My beloved mother, who genuinely cares for me, covered her face with her wrapper soaked in tears. Within her mind, she must have thought of the possibility of losing her first child to death after his university days. No one would have wished to experience such a calamity. The night was horrific for my family. No one expected the cruel deployment by the scheme."

This is a typical example of the consequences of the kinds of media representation that goes out to the public about specific places, which eventually leads to discrimination. Undoubtedly, the prospective corps member had already thought himself dead because of the information concerning that region of Nigeria.

The terrifying level of discrimination among the human race can also be traced to the false representation by various media organisations. With exaggerated news stories circulated across television stations, newspapers and social media platforms about the zone, the pictures of mass deaths have always been painted in the minds of thousands of people, particularly those residing in the Southern zone of the nation.

The pieces of discriminatory information are commonly associated with cases of violence, brutality, flagrant violation of human rights and jungle justice. The negative perception caused by this representation also contributed to Samuel's fears and doubts about his survival in the Northern state.

"Before I read the letter, I had never imagined travelling to any locations in the 19 Northern states due to the regular news claiming the mass death of the residents almost every day through insecurity largely sponsored by Boko Haram, banditry and other terrorist attacks. I used to wonder why many Nigerians still reside in the Northern region. I thought they preferred to die and suffer from insurgency and terrorism."

The narrator's statement cannot be overemphasised. A study by the Centre for Democracy and Development in 2019 also found that 59% of news articles connected with violence in Nigeria focus on the Northern region. This is repeatedly posted despite the unprecedented violence in the country. According to Amnesty International, the term "Fulani" appeared over 130 times in Nigerian media outlets within three months. Reportedly, this influences many Nigerians to portray the tribes negatively.

In a report presented by the Premium Times Centre for Investigative Journalism, Hausa and Fulani people were pictured as terrorists and criminals. Unfortunately, stories of remarkable achievements of great residents of the regions are not always given popularity and publicity. These ethnic stereotypes are displayed in the language adopted by the organisations where the Northerners struggle with imposed "backwardness" and "illiteracy."

Before Samuel received his call-up letter from the National Youth Service Commission, he had his fears about every Northern state in Nigeria. News from different media organisations claims that all northerners are in deadly zones. They are commonly associated with violence, brutality and jungle justice. This negative perception has continued to portray the tribe in a negative light, heightening the spread of negativity and terrorism.

"After accepting my fate, I was shocked by the outcome within two months. There was no single case of mass killing in my local government. Crimes were minimal. Everyone was relatively safe like other Southern parts of the country."

This is the reflection of the consequences of false media representation. Imagine being told that being posted to a particular location was a suicidal move. This orchestrates the decision of thousands of corps members posted to these stereotyped states to relocate to their preferred states as soon as possible. Some of them have to tell lies for their redeployment to any of the Southern states, which hinders the expectation to relate with other tribes in their states. The question is, how will this promote unity and oneness as originally proposed by the Federal Government, which led to the scheme's establishment after the Civil War?

The alarming level of discrimination against the Fulani can also be linked to popular headlines of Fulani herdsmen associated with criminality and terrorism. Even in the Southern parts of the country, several innocent individuals from the tribe were unjustly treated, prejudiced and stereotyped with criminal tendencies. With exaggerated news about the reports of banditry and abduction between 2015 and 2019, the media wrongly paints the picture of discrimination in people's minds. This continuously leads to harmful stereotypes as it also portrays certain tribes in a negative light, causing negativity and hatred.

Additionally, the publication of decisive messages used during election campaigns by politicians to win elections also leads to tension. Consequently, this negativity can lead to marginalisation and alienation, resulting in division against national unity. It is important to note that the media is hugely responsible for reinforcing prejudices and negativity.

This is also similar to the case of the Indigenous People of Biafra (IPOB), a group agitating for the secession of the South-East region from Nigeria. It is crucial to state that there were false media representations, as the group is being portrayed as a terrorist group. The exaggeration of the group's influence on media also affected the decision of many Nigerians to travel to the states, particularly on Mondays, due to the sit-at-home order allegedly imposed by the group.

AFRICAN MEDIA PORTRAYAL

A report generated by the Media Diversity Institute on African Media Portrayal of its continent raises some questions. Generally, Africa grapples with negative stereotypical news coverage ranging from stories on conflicts, kidnappings, xenophobia, irregular migration, famine, and corruption, among others. The truth is that the use of stereotypes against the continent has increased.

According to Violet Nakamba, a senior reporter at the Zambia Daily Mail, Africa is hugely represented negatively in the media because the outside world perceives it negatively. The article recommended always having a balanced article of both good and bad news of the continent to represent it well. Maybe they need to go and listen to and be well guided by Chimamanda Adichie's Ted Talk on "The dangers of a one-sided narrative."

In a research on the US Mass Media Portrayal of the African Continent, "The African Perspective" by Manya (2016), there are reports of the negative stories of hunger, poverty, and corruption as the most common types of news coverage on the US media. The results of fixed and existing stereotypes of Africa caused this. The results also proved that many Africans desired to share a lot of potential with the world if given the benefit of the doubt. The fact that there are many forms of negativity about the African continent does not erase the pieces of good news left unreported.

It is crucial to state that the negative images of Africa in the Western world can be traced to the adverse reports of the continent because most of them who had never visited the continent believed the reports. Many Africans have complained bitterly about the portrayal of the continent in a bad light, causing a negative impact on the continent.

THE ECONOMIC IMPACT OF MEDIA FALSE REPRESENTATION

The National Bureau of Statistics (NBS) found that the poverty rate in the country's Northern region is nearly twice that of the Southern region, with an estimated 76% of the population living below the poverty line. Also the economic condition of the Northern states is also evident in terms of GDP per capita, where the majority of these states are financially affected compared to their Southern counterparts.

Investors and business owners are also discouraged by the false representations of the affected zones, particularly the Northern states and their counterparts in the South East. By extension, this is also connected with the image of Nigeria before international organisations, as it has terrible consequences on the struggling economy. With the false belief that Nigeria is a hotbed of criminal activities, potential investors feel discouraged from investing in the country, hurting the economic growth.

Due to exaggerated news, negative stereotypes in Nigeria also affect the tourism industry. Many people negatively think that the country is unsafe. Many workers, especially civil and public servants, also believe the government is not encouraging them to thrive and achieve financial growth. This causes them to pursue opportunities elsewhere, causing brain drain after taking their expertise to other nations.

Additionally, the belief that Nigerian manufacturers produce poor-quality goods also causes trade imbalance. This is also capable of affecting the country's exportation ability.

The above reasons paint the country as untrustworthy by potential investors, economists and others.

UNITED STATES EXCLUSION ACTS AGAINST CHINESE CITIZENS

According to the Milestone, in the history of U.S. Foreign Relations, the Chinese Exclusion Act passed in the United States, signed by President Chester A. Arthur on May 6, 1882, provided a 10-year ban on Chinese labourers. Some immigrants who had relocated to the country were forced to obtain certifications. There are also reports of some Chinese who were refused citizenship. At the height of the exclusion, the act was extended for another ten years after its expiration in 1892. The acts were only repealed after China became a member of the Allied Nations during World War II in 1943.

The Indians are always prejudiced as mysterious and spiritual. Several myths about their spiritual prowess have always been passed from one generation to another. They are associated with mystical powers and charms connected with ancient Indian mythology.

Below are other examples of Indian stereotypes:

1. **Yoga**: It is believed that performing Yoga is a magical method of achieving sound health. Many people believe that the Indians practising Yoga tend to wield supernatural powers.

2. **VastuShastra**: This is an architectural system in India that is stereotyped as having mental properties.

3. **Ayurveda**: This medicine is stereotyped as the cure for every illness.

OTHER SERIOUS CONSEQUENCES OF NEGATIVE STEREOTYPES IN DIFFERENT COUNTRIES

The media coverage of the arrest of Raymond Igbalode Abbas, popularly known as Hushpuppi, who was sentenced to over 11 years in prison for his attempt to launder millions of dollars, also contributes negatively to the discrimination against Africans. The incident led to a damaging stereotype against the continent and Nigeria, affecting those working tirelessly to improve their lives. In some countries, Nigerians are tagged scammers, while others are always denied opportunities for housing and employment.

The negative perception that all Africans are into cyberbullying by some of the countries is also an example. This also made it extremely difficult for Nigerians to be taken seriously by the international community. There are stories of many tech workers who were denied job opportunities remotely due to this case.

This stigmatisation paints Africans as corrupt, leading to their struggle for acceptance into international scenes.

The media representation of stereotypes also leads to discrimination against African countries in cases where they were always thoroughly checked at the airport, excluding those from other countries. These stereotypes lead to suspicion against those from the blacklisted countries in the workplace, social gatherings and other areas. As a result of the stigmatisation, many Africans may continue to struggle with social isolation since they are tagged as fraudulent and corrupt.

Concerning racial profiling, it is imperative to state that different African countries faced stringent travel restrictions with rigorous visa application processes and scrutiny at the peak of Hushpuppi's case. Some individuals from the countries were denied entry and unnecessarily delayed.

Chapter Six

RELIGIOUS DISCRIMINATION AND PERSECUTION

Religious discrimination is an act of treating people harshly because of their religious practices, which is common all over the world, with cases of people of faith being marginalised, prosecuted and targeted for genocide. This is one of the major issues that have existed in the world. It is crucial to emphasise that religious discrimination manifests in various forms as it continues to harm people's lives. It occurs in different ways, which include Islamophobia, anti-Semitism, and Christophobia, among others. Unfortunately, all these can be demonstrated through microaggressions, stereotypes, persecution and hate expressions against the affected faith.

ISLAMOPHOBIA

This is regarded as the fear of Islam and Muslims. This also negatively affects Muslim communities all over the world, especially in locations where they are minorities. According to Bridge Initiative, Islamophobia is defined as the expression of hatred and extremism against Islam and Muslims, which results in social and political discrimination. The Organisation of Islamic Cooperation also explains Islamophobia as the expression of hatred, fear and prejudice against Islam through stigmatisation, racism and discrimination in the workplace, in media and in political spheres. In the article presented on the International Day to Combat Islamophobia by the United Nations, Islamophobia is defined as the hatred towards Muslims, which is targeted at the intimidation and harassment of Muslims, as it is always against anything that has to do with the symbols of being a Muslim.

In many countries all over the world, Muslims are often stereotyped with extremism and terrorism. This is evident in the perceptions of many individuals who believe that religion promotes violence. Unfortunately, this leads to surveillance and discrimination against the stereotyped individuals. In addition, many of them may also struggle with microaggressions when they receive provocative comments against their belief systems. In the vandalisation of their properties, their mosques may also be attacked by non-muslims in a bid to eradicate them.

The Christchurch Mosque Shooting, where 51 people were killed, which occurred in March 2019, is an example. According to reports online, the gunman targeted Muslims with an Islamophobia agenda. Critics also argued that Islamophobia sponsored the travel ban placed on citizens from several Muslim-majority communities. Amnesty International UK (2020) also reports that Former President Trump signed the executive order as many believed that the ban was inhumane as it remains a flagrant violation of human rights.

This also leads to discrimination in education and access to public service in countries where religious discrimination is evident. Reports emerged that Muslim women also suffered severe discrimination in France. The European Network Against Racism also states that there were many cases related to discrimination against Muslim women in France in employment or vocational studies. Further studies show that many were prohibited from wearing their religious symbols. In October 2023, Amnesty International also reported that the rules established regarding the use of sports head coverings were discriminatory against Muslim women players. This rule blatantly excluded women who wear head covers from participating in competitive matches, which violated their rights to health, private life, religion and expression. Jabhkiro (2022) also reports that the United Nations committee pointed out the discriminatory action against a France woman, known as Naima

Mezhoud, who was prevented from participating in vocational training because of her Islamic headscarf in 2010. It was also stated that the France Government banned the use of hijabs and other religious items in state schools. However, in a document on the religious violation, the United Nations Human Rights Committee ruled that the discrimination against Mezhoud is discrimination based on gender and religion.

THE IMPACTS OF ISLAMOPHOBIA

1. Due to the occurrence of hatred towards the religion, its faithful may suffer from mental challenges caused by illnesses and depression. They may also battle social exclusion since they are always tagged as extremists and violent.

According to Young Minds, the research on Islamophobia showed that over 78% of Muslim youths have battled Islamophobia in their lifetimes. The Times, on The Devastating Mental Health Effects of Islamophobia, confirms that there were sudden cases of the rise of this generalisation on people assumed in Czech, which, by extension, hurt the Muslim communities in the United States and all over the world.

The dangerous effects of this could affect their mental health, causing low confidence or self-esteem. Furthermore, their lives may be threatened, causing them to fear and struggle for safety.

2. Due to unjustifiable discrimination, many Muslims may lose job opportunities because of the stereotyped mindsets

of the employers of labour. This may be demonstrated during job interviews. The employed may also be victims of delayed promotion and toxicity in the workplace. With this negative perception about them and the assumption that they are violent, they may never be treated respectfully.

3. Lack of respect for human choices may also affect women who dress according to the tenets of the faith. They may be subjected to all forms of sexual harassment and abuse, probably caused by their mode of dressing or identity. This played in the example given above about France, which made laws forbidding them from appearing in their preferred mode of dressing. This was also regarded as one of the religious discrimination against humanity that should never be accepted. Discrimination is indeed a war against humanity.

Fighting all forms of religious discrimination is the responsibility of everyone. It involves protesting against political, personal and social discrimination. It is also important to emphasise that all forms of religious discrimination are flagrant violations of the fundamentals of human freedom to worship or perform any religious activities. Sitting on the fence is also not enough. It is necessary to embark on aggressive sensitisation towards fighting the threat against humanity and make life a haven for everyone, regardless of their chosen religions. The above practical solutions are not limited to the countries where Muslims are affected; it is also for all nations, including Muslim-dominated ones, reiterating the value of respect for all religions.

CHRISTIANS AND THEIR PERSECUTION

Despite the estimated population of 2.4 billion adherents all over the world, Christians are also affected by brutal religious discrimination on account of their faith. Some have been subjugated to all forms of politically motivated persecution, including economic reasons depending on the reasons for persecution. This is also common in some countries known for their discrimination and extremism, such as Iraq and Pakistan. In these Muslim-dominated countries, the minority struggle to practice their religious beliefs due to the recognised cases of persecution.

In Nigeria, there are reports of communities attacked by extremist and misguided believers of the religion. In a news story released by the Punch (2024), the Executive Director of the Muslim Rights Concern, Professor Ishaq Akintola, expressed his dissatisfaction with the attacks in Plateau State in January 2024. This level of atrocity destroyed two churches and eight mosques, leading to the death of more than 30 individuals. The security situation in the area caused many people, primarily women and children, to relocate for their lives. The Voice of America (2009) also reported the attacks on Christians in Jigawa State following a blasphemous statement uttered by a Christian woman against Prophet Muhammed. The overzealous miscreants sponsored the destruction of churches and shops allegedly owned by Christians.

According to the Media Organisation, in 2009, at least 15,000 people have been affected by communal, ethnic and religious violence in the country since the return to democracy. The report given by Independent Newspaper (2010) also stated that a church filled with worshippers was also razed down by angry Muslim youths in Jos, resulting in the death of 27 people and 300 reported cases of wounds in the religious violence. Plateau State, one of the states in the Northern region, is notorious for its common cases of religious violence. This is attributed to local disputes among themselves, which led to the death of more than 1000 people in September 2001 and more than 700 lives in 2004 in a Muslim-Christian battle for supremacy.

According to the House of Common Library on Religious Persecution and the Watch List in 2024, below are the reports generated for 2023 after the assessment of violent incidences on private, family, community, national and church lives.

Approximately, close to 365 million Christians are subjected to extreme discrimination.

Considering the level of persecution, 1 in 7 Christians suffered from persecution worldwide. In Africa, 1 in 5 were observed and 1 in 7 in Asia.

90% of those who lost their lives to religious violence as Christians were traced to Nigeria. All over the world, it was gathered that 4,998 Christians feared death for faith-related issues. Concerning faith-related deaths in the world, 3,621 people died in 2023, 5,898 died in 2022, and 4,761 lost their lives in 2021.

Regarding the destruction of Christians' properties, it was also reported that 14,766 churches and Christians were attacked in persecution and other cases of religious violence.

The highest rate of reported persecution cases was also traced to North Korea, Somalia, Libya, Eritrea and Yemen.

The Global Christian Relief also presented the disheartening stories of Christians who suffered persecution and intense discrimination attributed to their faith in Jesus Christ. It was also reported that many of them were displaced from their homes and harassed by mob violence. With false accusations of blasphemy, a lot of them also battled assault, martyrdom and kidnappings.

Peter (2004), in his article e, also explains that there are some countries where Christianity is forbidden and restricted. Even though the laws against practising the religion were not passed, the persecution of Christians in these countries is still in existence, such as North Korea, which upholds the freedom of religion in their constitutions with contradictory actions against

Christians who were targeted for their religion. He also argued that the legal recognition of the religion does not necessarily guide against the persecution of Christians all over the world.

In Afghanistan, the conversion of any Muslim commonly leads to severe punishments, including death, due to the country's stringent laws. The Christians there have to practise their religious beliefs with secrecy and battle the consequences if caught. It was reported that the extreme persecution is not only caused by the insensitivity of the Taliban-led central government but also by local communities and family members.

North Korea is also classified as one of the most dangerous places for Christians all over the world. It was also reported that the use of the Bible, especially in public places, leads to imprisonment in labour camps and other forms of punishment. The Christians are also detained without any opportunities for trials, with their families in the harsh consequences.

In Somalia, the country is also recognised for its refusal to acknowledge any other religion apart from Islam. Reports also suggest that there are deadly consequences for the conversion of any Muslim to Christianity, which includes their execution by Islamist militant groups established for the eradication of Christianity.

There are also reports of increased Islamic extremism in Yemen, particularly against Christians from immigrant communities.

The attack on the religious institutions and gatherings makes it extremely dangerous for the adherents to practice their faith openly.

Only recognised Christian denominations are also allowed to practise Christianity in Eritrea. Reports also suggest that independent Christian denominations battle stringent persecution as their members are subjected to all forms of inhumane treatment and arrest. It is also disheartening to state that some are detained in shipping containers.

In Nigeria, blasphemy laws are pretentiously used to attack Christians. This is common in the Northern states where Sharia laws are implemented. It is important to mention that the Southern part of the country experiences religious tolerance compared to the North, where churches are frequently attacked, leading to the death of many Christians.

Pakistan is also notorious for the blasphemy laws enacted to target Christians, which are majorly used to cause mob violence. There are also indications that the Christians living in the country struggle with systemic discrimination. Death sentences can also be caused by the accusation of blasphemy, making it uneasy for the Christian community to survive.

Converting from Islam in Iran is also lethal despite the fact that Christianity is tolerated to an extent, particularly among historical Armenian and Assyrian communities. Christians are often restricted from preaching their faith to non-Christians as they are likely to face arbitrary arrests and persecution.

The call for anti-conversion laws in some states in India can also be regarded as a threat that affects the Christian community in the country. At the same time, it is known that the country's constitution guarantees religious freedom. The anti-Christian policies make it difficult to implement the fundamental freedom of religion.

North Korea and Saudi Arabia are also recognised for the enactment of strict bans on the possession and importation of religious texts other than state-approved ones. The violation of the bans can lead to imprisonment or other worse punishments. There are also cases of places where owning a Bible is illegal. These policies pose a daunting challenge to the need for every human to believe in any religion of their choice.

Chapter Seven

THE HUMAN COST OF DIVISION

....

"As long as people can be judged by the colour of their skin, the problem is not solved."
– Oprah Winfrey

THE PERSONAL AND SOCIETAL CONSEQUENCES OF RACISM AND DISCRIMINATION

MEDICAL DISADVANTAGE:

Health disparities can also affect those experiencing racism, especially when they lack access to quality health services. This case of racism and discrimination is also likely to increase their chances of having health challenges. In a viral video on Tiktok, the content creator discussed medical racism as the systemic, biased and discriminatory practices that impact the healthcare of marginalised communities. She also revealed that a study has shown that 50% of medical students and residents have false beliefs about biological differences between Black and White patients. These false beliefs include the idea that Black people's skin is thicker, their blood coagulates more quickly, or they have fewer nerve endings than White people. On High Black maternal mortality rates: black women are three times more likely to die during childbirth, and in some places, this rate is as high as seven times.

Additionally, there are medical equations that treat Black people differently. For example, there is an equation that assumes all Black patients have better kidney functioning than any other race, which is based on the false belief that Black patients have higher muscle mass. This lie was used to justify slavery. This equation has made it harder for Black patients to get kidney transplants. It's racism, plain and simple. This equation was finally changed only in 2021.

EDUCATIONAL DISADVANTAGE: It is unfortunate to state that the victims of racism are usually given limited opportunities for professional development. This can also result in lower academic achievements and unequal access to resources.

CAREER DISADVANTAGE: In countries where racism has gained domination, the disadvantaged may have limited job opportunities and lower wages, causing them to feel economically defeated as second-class citizens.

SOCIAL DIVISION AND ISOLATION: Affected individuals also suffer from social exclusion. This also affects their ability to network and form quality relationships with others in their countries of residence. It will also affect their active engagement in community activities. An extreme case is often seen where the government looks the other way as communities concentrated with minority ethnic groups rot away and continue to suffer from deprivation of essential public services like security and sanitation. I perceive that the happenings in places like Bradford in the UK, where street and highway begging is the order of the day, is a graphic representation of the above claim, wildly contrasting what is obtainable nationally. It's like the authorities had a meeting to decide, "You know what, let's allow them to mess up the whole place and self-destruct; after all, they're the ones to reap the consequences of their actions." Yet again, maybe it's another wild thinking of mine or perception (which, of course, isn't always reality). But what if it is in this particular case?

DISREGARD FOR HUMAN RIGHTS: Obviously, discrimination and racism have no regard for the fundamental principles of equality and human rights.

THE EMOTIONAL AND PSYCHOLOGICAL IMPACTS ON VICTIMS

Anxiety, depression and trauma are the psychological effects of racism and discrimination. Cogburn et al. (2024) also noted that black individuals in the United States experience morbidity from mental illnesses due to racism. Factors such as European imperialism, enslavement, the myth of Black inferiority, and scientific racial classification have perpetuated disparities, leading to the underestimation, misdiagnosis, and inadequate treatment of mental illness in Black populations.

Mark Rowland, Chief Executive of the Mental Health Foundation, has released a statement that claims racism is a mental health issue. Richard (2023) reported in The Washington Post that research shows racial discrimination is linked to mental health issues such as depression, anxiety, PTSD, hypertension, and obesity. It has also been reported that Black Americans are twice as likely to develop dementia compared to White Americans. Further research indicates that racism speeds up the ageing process and can lead to the damage of critical brain circuits responsible for regulating emotions and cognition.

According to Williams (2015) in The New York Times Magazine, race-based stress and trauma are the psychological effects of racism that minority groups regularly face. These effects can manifest as symptoms such as depression, inability to sleep, anger, loss of appetite, apathy, avoidance, and emotional numbing.

Kamaldeep (2018) also states that there is a connection between racism and discrimination, which can lead to experiences of hallucinations and delusions. This means that when people face discrimination based on their race, they may begin to have false experiences that are not real.

Trauma has been identified as a crucial topic to be discussed in conversations centred on racism. The effects of trauma can be profound, particularly when experienced by minority groups, resulting in long-lasting psychological impacts. Racial trauma, or race-based traumatic stress (RBTS), refers to the mental and emotional injury caused by encounters with racial bias and ethnic discrimination, racism and hate crimes. Any individual who has experienced an emotionally painful, sudden and uncontrollable racist encounter is at the risk of suffering from a race-based traumatic stress injury. In the US, Black Indigenous People of Colour (BIPOC) are most vulnerable due to living under a system of white supremacy.

WAYS PREJUDICE HINDERS SOCIAL PROGRESS AND ECONOMIC OPPORTUNITIES

Career Discrimination: Unprofessional hiring managers also practice prejudice. This deprives those struggling with racism of opportunities for professional and financial growth. It also leads to ineffective productivity for organisational growth.

Political Marginalisation: Discrimination and racism also hugely contribute to the gross underrepresentation of certain groups in governance. This marginalisation leads to underdevelopment of the areas where the people's needs are ignored.

Housing Discrimination: In this case, the victims of racism are usually denied the opportunities to reside in quality accommodation and access to economic opportunities.

I watched a video of a White man who pretended to be blind and was walking across the road. Many people offered to help and guide him. Similarly, an African pretended to be blind and moved across the same road. Sadly, no one was willing to help the Black man. Funnily enough, these people may be acting on the false information that they have gotten concerning Africans. As a primary school student, I thought that every Asian was Chinese. In my little mind, once you looked Asian, you were from China. I later discovered that Asia had other countries aside from China. So, there was this child in my school who looked Chinese, and I immediately thought that he would be good at martial arts. I believed that since veterans like Jackie Chan and Bruce Lee were Chinese and were good with martial arts. Well, I was wrong. In the same vein, making generalisations can lead to wrong conclusions.

People are different and should be treated as individuals. They should not be labelled based on where they are from. It will be delightful to see individuals come out of the generalisation, racist mindset. I caught something on MSM news about Idris Elba declining to take the role of James Bond because of nasty comments about his race. One may think that as celebrities, they are immune from discrimination. Unfortunately, people (celebrity or not) miss out on opportunities, too, as a result of racial discrimination. Some societies are yet to grow out of it collectively and mature to a point where racial discrimination does not matter. There are places in the present-day UK where people give you a suspicious look, and you can practically feel it. This is an example of the unconscious bias I spoke about earlier.

TRUE LIFE STORY OF THOSE AFFECTED BY RACISM AND DISCRIMINATION

According to the Guardian, on March 14, 2023, a woman named Eleanor Williams was jailed for eight years after lying about being raped by three Asian white men. The news report also has it that one Jordan Trengove spent 73 days in prison after being falsely accused of raping and drugging her at gun points. These allegations levelled against them almost made them attempt suicide.

Steve Ndukwu, in his YouTube video, also narrated how immigration officials treated Black Africans. He shared the experience he had with customs officials on one of his trips when only the blacks were stopped and searched thoroughly. A lot of people decided not to travel back to the country due to the level of embarrassment they faced, excluding white men. One of the Tanzanian students also discussed how her bags were searched before the officer suggested she should come to the country with her diplomatic passport. She wondered why they would not have searched her bags if she had presented her diplomatic passport. In her words, "I did not see it as racism; I see it as discrimination."

In a tweet on X, Chude Nnamdi complained about the discrimination in Poland, where Nigerians cannot open accounts with the bank he visited. He discovered this after his unsuccessful attempt to open an account for his child. He wondered why the bank banned Nigerians from opening accounts. However, this does not justify the level of discrimination demonstrated due to the possible offence of some Nigerians. That is discrimination, and it should not exist at all.

DANGERS OF MAKING GENERALISATIONS

I remember one time, my 8-year-old son came back from school gloomy. After probing, I found out that the mood was because he felt no one wanted to be his friend in his class. I had to find a way to calm him down and reassure him that the fact that he felt that way didn't mean it was correct. I made him realise that he was new to the school and that making friends could take some time. I tried hard to make him dispel the notion that everyone was deliberately shunning him or that there was some form of gang up against him.

I was vindicated when, a few weeks after that incident, he and just a handful of boys in his class were invited to the birthday party of not just one person in his class but twins. My son was very excited knowing that some people wanted to be his friend and expressed it by specially selecting those to attend their birthday party. I'm glad he has learned the lesson not to be quick to jump to conclusions, especially when it's just based on feelings which might be wrong or right.

That's what happens when I hear or see people making generalisations. How can you label everyone from a specific place as wrong just because someone from that place was mean to you? No two humans are the same. We have our unique ID in the form of DNA. People from a specific place can exhibit some particular behaviour, but it's not always the case. Often, generalising or prejudice stems from unhealed wounds of past offences or incidents. A case in point is where some persons of Igbo extraction in Nigeria still harbour grudges against the Hausa/Fulani because of the pogrom against their people that led to the Civil War. Not only that, even the Yorubas are not left out because of a particular army officer of Yoruba origin who betrayed the Biafran cause. That's why some Igbo persons refer to the Yorubas as traitors and people who can't be trusted.

It is important that, as humans, we are mindful of our actions because every person from our village, town, state and country would be labelled as the wrong or right we do. Whether we know it or not, we are ambassadors or representatives of our origin. Through us, people can confirm whatever assumptions (negative or positive) they already harbour about people from our locality or origin. For instance, the issue of corruption (which, by the way, is a sin) can be attributed to any particular country as it exists everywhere. It's just that its prevalence differs from place to place. So, the fact that someone from country A was found by the court to be corrupt isn't enough justification to label everyone from that country as a corrupt person or have the tendency to be corrupt.

How about violence or crime? I've watched many movies where the antagonists (or what we popularly refer to as the bad guys) happen to be Albanian. It's hard for me not to think of any Albanian I meet as being a mean person or having a tendency to do drugs or get involved in crime, which, by the way, isn't correct. However, I must admit that I almost concluded my theory of the Albanians when one of my former colleagues, who is Albanian, was trying to psyche me into his world by saying: "I had a mate that was Nigerian, and he was cool. We used to run things together, like dealing drugs and stuff. We even got into a car chase with the police, and I was lucky not to get caught." I could easily conclude my theory that Albanians have a thirst for crime based on this guy, but that wouldn't be right. Just like he assumed, because I'm Nigerian, I should tend to deal with drugs, but he got it all wrong. There are so many things people make generalisations about, like attitude (including behaviour, kindness, politeness, etc), sexual behaviour, punctuality, marriage (like saying men from certain places don't make good fathers or women from certain areas are good wives), the list goes on.

We should all be careful about various generalisations because they affect how we treat and relate to people. That's what usually leads to profiling. Recent studies show that an African American youth has a higher likelihood of being arrested and jailed than other tribes in America. This can be seen in the inmate figures across the US and the high proportion of African Americans in the prisons.

FACTORS THAT CONTRIBUTE TO AMERICAN RACISM

According to Steve (2020), racism is defined as a pandemic and established system of exploitation based on race, which is prevalent in the United States. Robert and Rizzo reviewed the seven factors responsible for the prevalence of racism in America. One of the first three factors reviewed are categories, which includes the division of humans into different discriminated groups; factions, which arouses in group loyalty and intergroup competition; and segregation, which encourages racist perceptions and beliefs. The research also recognises that children are familiar with the faces of the racial majority group, with the fact that black children recognise white faces better than how white children recognise black faces, and this could potentially lead to issues in the world.

The remaining reviewed factors include media, which heightens the supremacy of White Americans through overrepresentation in the marginalisation of people of colour; passivism, which is about the denial of the existence of discrimination; and power, which is responsible for the legality of racism on both micro and macro levels. According to the scholars responsible for the identification of these factors, the most harmful is passive racism, which is being apathetic towards racism, including the denial of its existence.

EQUITY NOT DIVERSITY

Equity refers to the fair treatment, access, opportunity, and advancement for all people while striving to eliminate barriers that have prevented the full participation of some groups. At the same time, diversity, on the other hand, is the presence of differences within a particular setting.

Equity is a better solution to the challenges of racism, prejudice and discrimination because it allows for inclusive leadership, a marginalised educational system, and fair allocation of resources. While diversity will improve the challenges caused by racism and prejudice, equity will help solve the menace.

In a TEDx talk by Paloma Media, she emphasised the need to stop discussing diversity, which is common. In her illustration, she invited her audience to a house party. They were people of diverse cultures and tribes; what was important was how everyone would be treated as it challenges our system, which can be daunting. There is a need to swap out diversity and embrace workplace equity through racial and gender representations by 50% in a specified number of years.

Chapter Eight

DISMANTLING THE WALLS: STRATEGIES FOR CHANGE

"Friendship doesn't recognise colour. Isolation does."
– **June Stoyer**

COMBATING PREJUDICE AND DISCRIMINATION: PRACTICAL SOLUTIONS FOR INDIVIDUALS

Nations and organisations must embrace diversity, equity and inclusion policies until it becomes a culture. They should not pretend to be imbibing it, while in reality, it is just lip service or playing to the gallery. In some countries like Nigeria, tribal sentiments remain fundamental to contesting and winning elections. In the last general elections, rather than focus on the candidates' manifestoes and policy issues. Many chose to play the primordial politics of ethnicity and religion.

If only they knew that poverty, crime and economic deprivation know no tribe. It is another display of ignorance. The fact that someone hails from your hometown or village is no guarantee that they'll prioritise it while in office. Even if they chose to prioritise it, it still isn't right. If that's the case, then every constituency should push forward their candidate to ensure they are a top priority when they get there. This is not the way a society should run. The interest of the entire area of coverage of their office should be top on their agenda. Fairness and equitable distribution of resources should be paramount.

While a policy like the Federal character in Nigeria is good, some aspects must be amended. This policy aims to promote national unity by mandating that Federal job vacancy slots, political appointments and other opportunities be spread equitably among the federating units. Its flaws include promoting laziness and docility in zones that are behind economically or educationally. A case in point is where university admissions exam cut-off marks are lower in Northern Nigeria than in their Southern counterparts. If poorly managed, it can further tear the country apart instead of uniting it. It is designed for constitutional needs to be amended where necessary to ensure people don't assume office and go on a nepotistic campaign of filling up positions with only people of their tribe. If multi-tribal villages, towns, cities and the country don't see themselves as one, why should you expect to be treated fairly and accepted in another country? You'd better pick the log in your eye before pointing out the one in someone else's.

THE IMPORTANCE OF SELF-AWARENESS AND RECOGNISING PERSONAL BIASES

When Socrates said, "Man, know thyself," he probably didn't know it would later metamorphose into the study of emotional intelligence, where self-awareness is integral. We should understand and appreciate our unique features and embrace our limitations. We live in a funny world where, like a Yoruba adage says, "The one with a head but has no cap wishes he's got one, while the one with no head but has a cap wishes he's got a head." The moral of the adage is that none of us is perfect. When you accept this reality, you will never wish you were someone else. You will never contemplate changing anything about you just to become like someone else. Now, I'm not condemning admiring other people or having role models that we look up to. However, we should only emulate some parts because they also do not have it all figured out. Social media makes some people look like they've got perfect lives. It's all a ruse; everyone, yes, I mean everyone, even celebrities, have deltas or gaps, too, i.e. things they wish they could have or someone they want to they could also be like.

I've never felt comfortable changing your skin tone/colour for any reason, probably because I understand the biology behind the skin. What makes our skin darker or lighter is a pigment called the melanin gland." Using creams containing hydroquinone attacks this pigment, turning a dark-skinned person into a light-skinned. It sounds theoretically accessible, but it does not happen so fast, and it has serious health repercussions. I perceive that some people do this because of their disdain for their skin colour. They've been made to believe that "black" connotes "bad", so they can't wait to switch to the "light" and become "light skinned." It's not impossible that religion could also be responsible for this anomaly. Christianity (which, by the way, is a way of life and not necessarily a religion), portrays the Lord and Savior, Jesus, as "white" (fair-skinned) through statues and pictures. In contrast, the evil one, Satan, is portrayed as "black." This narrative makes it easy to conclude that anything white is good while black is terrible.

So, it's beyond the physical actions of someone changing their skin colour but has much to do with their psychological state. Someone once said that it's easier to free someone from slavery physically but not mentally. The slave era ended a long time ago, but sadly, many are yet to get emancipated from mental slavery. Otherwise, how do you explain why some people today believe they're inferior to others just because they were once their colonial masters? It'll require a great deal of education and enlightenment to get such a person out of the state they're in.

Growing up, we were warned against speaking our native languages in nursery, primary and secondary schools. They were termed "vernacular", and if you were caught speaking it, you'd get into serious trouble with the teachers and school administration. Cambridge Dictionary defines Vernacular as "the form of a language that a particular group of speakers use naturally, especially in informal situations." Back then, I didn't know the word's meaning, but it usually sounded like a taboo. That made our native languages look unattractive, thereby promoting just the use of the English language. Please don't get me wrong; I'm not saying learning to communicate in one of the most spoken languages worldwide is terrible, but it should not be at the expense of one's heritage and culture. The effect of "vernacularising" one's native language is unquantifiable. One of which is that some languages are now going extinct because parents are not passing it on to their children; cultural dressing isn't left out, too. Some people have lost their sense of identity just because they've adopted other cultures and ditched theirs. I find it awkward whenever I see someone wear a native Yoruba dress like "Agbada" and crown it with a fez cap with sneakers to match. That's my definition of a confused person. Trying to infuse two highly different cultures in the name of fashion should be done cautiously so you don't lose the essence of people's culture as it's their identity.

Another disturbing one is human hair. If you're born with straight or curled hair, be thankful to your creator. I've seen some Nigerian women spend a tremendous amount of money to procure synthetic attachment called "bone-straight" or "Brazilian hair", all in the name of beauty. I know everyone has a right to spend their money on whatever they wish. I only ask that they check that their reason for going that length is not because they hate that they were born with short curly hair, which can be best fit for afro, braids and countless plait styles. My point is you are beautiful as you are; don't kill yourself trying to be like someone else.

Some celebrities, living and dead, have tried to change their physical features via plastic surgery, but it didn't end well for them. Shockingly, some of the parts changed are the nose, lips, butts and so on. Having a good knowledge of yourself will allow anyone to embrace their roots and culture regardless of where they are. However, people may want to develop some personal biases because of their experiences with someone of the same descent. However, you can change the narrative by being a good ambassador of your culture. The emergence of Barack Obama as the president of America did a lot to re-orient so many people in America about the African race. The problem of personal biases in the culture of people cannot be solved overnight; however, with continuous advocacy, the mindset of people can be changed.

I try as often as possible to be a good ambassador of Nigeria; I am a proud Nigerian, and it doesn't matter how long I spend elsewhere. I will never forget my roots. I believe strongly that it is imposter syndrome that will cause a person to try to be like someone else or act like someone else. Why will I fake my accent to sound British or American? Interestingly, even in Britain, the accents are not the same. The Scots speak in a different accent from the Irish; similarly, those from Northern Ireland speak in a different accent from those from Liverpool. These nationalities are never shy of speaking in their accent. This is sadly not the case with many Africans; we are not always proud of our accents. I often encourage Africans to be natural; just be yourself!

I believe in my potential as a Nigerian; I am so proud of where I come from and proud of my name, Adetunji Banwo. My name has a meaning. I tell people to feel free to call me Tunji or my nickname, T.J., if they think Adetunji is tongue twisting. In some cases, I teach people how to pronounce my name. How do I pronounce German names like Schwarz or Arnold Schwarzenegger or a term like Volkswage if I am not taught how to? I may not pronounce it exactly like the Germans, but I will try to pronounce their names to the best of my abilities.

I choose the name I want to be addressed by, and I go the extra mile to teach people how to call it. So, it would help if you did not allow people to choose what to call you; neither should you be scared that your name will be mispronounced.

Chapter Nine

THE POWER OF EDUCATION AND ADVOCACY

"Prejudice is an opinion without judgement."
– Voltaire

THE ROLE OF EDUCATION IN DISMANTLING PREJUDICE AND PROMOTING TOLERANCE

It is crucial to state that the role of education in dismantling prejudice and promoting tolerance cannot be overemphasised. This attempt will reorient individuals, help them comprehensively understand diversity, and challenge preconceived information about other races or individuals. This can also arm learners with the skills required to question assumptions and challenge age-long biases against the victims of racism and discrimination. Undoubtedly, education will play a profound role in advocating oneness, humanity and empathy for others.

When individuals from different backgrounds or continents meet, education fosters connectivity, collaboration and networking skills. It helps them brainstorm and work collectively on projects. With quality education, individuals can be trained on fundamental human rights and explain why everyone must embrace equity among ourselves. Therefore, the government needs to invest heavily in education to achieve the goal of advocating tolerance and challenging all forms of negativity and racism against others.

Education can also be used to dispel myths and stereotypes to emphasise the importance of respecting our diversity as humans. It is also important to equip the youths with the skills needed to excel in the 21st century towards ensuring inclusiveness. Also, teachers should be mandated to promote inclusiveness through effective classroom management without any room for discrimination.

ENCOURAGING OPEN DIALOGUE IN SCHOOLS AND COMMUNITIES ABOUT RACE AND EQUALITY

From the classroom to the community, strategic teachings can be taught to create an inclusive society. The role of education as a catalyst for change cannot be underestimated. It can be a powerful tool to transform generational mindsets and social norms. Dialogue about race and equality should be enforced to ensure the appreciation of our differences as humans. The following are the strategies that can be adopted:

- Empathy and understanding of others' perspectives should be taught to enhance the unity among all humans regardless of their nationalities. This will also break down the walls of discrimination. This can also be improved by incorporating topics on race and equality into various school subjects such as Civic Education, History, Social studies and others.
- Students should always be encouraged to engage in open discussions about the danger of racial discrimination. This will also help them reduce the chances of forming stereotyped attitudes.
- Enough educational materials for the enlightenment of the public should be used.
- Plans on diversity should be implemented to fight against all forms of discrimination.

It's a fight of good against evil or light against darkness. We must not allow ourselves to be caught up in the wrong side of humanity and history by being racist or doing/saying nothing when something happens around us that we're aware of. A quote that has influenced me dramatically says, "Posterity will judge us for the problems we created, the ones we solved and/or the ones we saw and ignored." Please do what you can within your circle of influence to promote diversity, equality and inclusion of all persons irrespective of their tribe, gender or skin colour.

96

Chapter Ten

THE PLACE OF LAW AND POLICY

"Justice is truth in action."
– Benjamin Disraeli

ANALYSING THE EFFECTIVENESS OF EXISTING ANTI-DISCRIMINATION LAWS AND POLICIES

One significant recommendation for combating discrimination and prejudice in society is the need for governments to set clear punishments for violators. The process might be challenging, but it will play an important role in promoting justice for everyone. It is also important to provide opportunities for resolving disputes to encourage accountability among institutions and individuals.

An excerpt from the US Department of Justice, Civil Rights Division, Federal Protections Against National Origin Discrimination reads:

"Federal laws prohibit discrimination based on a person's national origin, race, colour, religion, disability, sex, and familial status. Laws prohibiting national origin discrimination make it illegal to discriminate because of a person's birthplace, ancestry, culture or language. This means people cannot be denied equal opportunity because they or their family are from another country, because they have a name or accent associated with a national origin group, because they participate in certain customs associated with a national origin group, or because they are married to or associate with people of a certain national origin."

Having the right laws to protect from being racially abused and deter anyone from perpetrating the act is a step in the right direction. This is what every government around the world should ensure. Otherwise, racially motivated hate crimes will continue to plague.

There is a need for ongoing legal reform and enforcement mechanisms. A lot needs to be done to address the skewed nature of the criminal justice system. Justice must not only be perceived to be done but be done. Security agencies must be given adequate training on the subject of DEI to help stamp out racial profiling.

ADVOCATING FOR POLICIES PROMOTING DIVERSITY AND INCLUSION IN INSTITUTIONS

The National Youth Service Corps Act introduced by the Nigerian government in 1973 is very laudable and should be emulated globally to foster national unity and social integration among its people. However, it's not a job for the government alone but also for civil organisations and NGOs. Civil organisations must engage in societal sensitisation on the importance of promoting diversity.

Bishop Mattew Kukah on Arise TV lamented the level of ethnic jingoism in Nigerian universities. He recalled that there was a time when the universities had lectures from various lecturers worldwide. Unfortunately, today, there is hardly any federal university where the vice chancellor is not an indigene of the hosting community. This is traceable to the inability to manage diversity in the institutions.

Lamenting further on religious discrimination, he asked why a place of worship should be a problem to the northern universities. The universities in the northern region have refused to implement the recommendation of the National Universities Commission (NUC) on the building of places of worship in the universities.

Speaking further on the recruitment process, he stated that it is now based on "who you know." Certificates are no longer relevant. The federal government needs to look into this issue for national inclusion urgently.

ENCOURAGING READERS TO HOLD INSTITUTIONS ACCOUNTABLE FOR DISCRIMINATORY PRACTICES

With effective whistle-blowing policies and a fair governance system, people will be encouraged to speak out whenever there's a case of racial discrimination. Easy and toll-free numbers can be made available just like 911 for emergencies. An example of this that readily comes to mind is a write-up by the British Transport Police; it reads, "If you see something that doesn't seem right, call the British Transport Police. See It, Say It, Sorted."

The decision by the English Football Association to include the slogan "No room for racism" is also laudable and very symbolic in tackling the menace of racism in the game of football and, indirectly, the country at large.

Chapter Eleven

LOVE: THE ANTIDOTE TO HATE

"An eye for an eye makes the world blind."
– Mahatma Gandhi

THE POWER OF LOVE IN OVERCOMING PREJUDICE AND BUILDING BRIDGES

The movie "Pocahontas" comes to mind whenever I think of love as the vital bridge-building material regarding racism. It shows how powerful love can be in building bridges and connecting us. We all want to love and be loved.

The lyrics of the song "Colours of the Wind" by Judy Kuhn explain the importance of love and acceptance in our world. Furthermore, it encourages the need to stop discrimination.

"You think I'm an ignorant savage

And you've been so many places

I guess it must be so

But still, I cannot see

If the savage one is me

How can there be so much that you don't know?

You don't know

You think you own whatever land you land on

The Earth is just a dead thing you can claim

But I know every rock and tree and creature

Has a life, has a spirit, has a name

You think the only people who are people

Are the people who look and think like you

But if you walk the footsteps of a stranger

You'll learn things you never knew, you never knew

Have you ever heard the wolf cry to the blue corn moon?

Or asked the grinning bobcat why he grinned?

Can you sing with all the voices of the mountain?

Can you paint with all the colours of the wind?

Can you paint with all the colours of the wind?

Come run the hidden pine trails of the forest

Come taste the sun sweet berries of the Earth

Come roll in all the riches all around you

And for once, never wonder what they're worth

The rainstorm and the river are my brothers

The heron and the otter are my friends

And we are all connected to each other
In a circle, in a hoop that never ends
How high does the sycamore grow?
If you cut it down, then you'll never know
And you'll never hear the wolf cry to the blue corn moon
For whether we are white or copper skinned
We need to sing with all the voices of the mountain
We need to paint with all the colours of the wind
You can own the Earth and still
All you'll own is Earth until
You can paint with all the colours of the wind."

Love knows no boundaries, indeed. I recently attended the wedding of one of my cousins based in Canada while her fiance lives in the UK. I understand they connected virtually and courted until it crescendoed to marriage. I'm so happy for them because they didn't let tribal differences affect their love. He's of the Igbo tribe, while our family is of the Yoruba tribe in Nigeria. Back in the day, it would have been impossible to achieve this feat. Even villages sharing borders sometimes warn their children not ever to consider marrying anyone from the next village, not to talk about a faraway one and a different tribe at that. This shows how many have become enlightened and overcome tribal sentiments when choosing who to marry (or should I say when they become a slave of love).

One of the solutions that can be an aid to cure the problem of racism, discrimination, tribalism, and all that looks like it, in all shapes and forms, is for us to bond, whether by marriage or as a team in the organisation or neighbours in the same society. When we build a strong bond, light will eventually overcome darkness. Good will overcome evil. Imagine a home where the children are mixed tribes for a moment; I don't see them preferring one tribe over the other. They'll likely love the tribes equally since that runs in their blood. It's like separating yourself into two parts that can't work, right?

Interestingly, this marriage of inconvenience has been around for a long time and has been used to settle feuds between warring groups, communities, empires and kingdoms. Something like this played out in the series "The Peaky Blinders", where the same Irish guy hated by the Peaky Blinders because of his involvement with the IRA ended up marrying their sister and even consummated their union with a child. That was a defining moment for the peaky blinders as they had to drop all plans to kill the guy, seeing he's now a member of their family, plus it'll hurt their sister. That's what blood connections can do to us. The point here is we should never allow tribe or religion or mundane stuff like skin colour to be our criteria in marriage or partnership. Inter-ethnic or inter-cultural marriage can help in combating racism and nailing it to the coffin perpetually.

The world needs more love, not hate. Humans will always slide into fighting and wars as long as racism, discrimination, and tribalism thrive. So, I'm hoping this book will be an eye-opener to individuals, policymakers, and leaders that love is what we need to combat the issue of racism.

We must appreciate and understand our diversity as humans to live in harmony. We need variety in the world as variety is the spice of life. If everyone in the world were from one tribe, I can imagine it would be such a boring place, so we should embrace diversity and not try to make anyone feel inferior to us.

EXPLORING THE CONCEPT OF UNCONDITIONAL ACCEPTANCE

If we were to dig up the offences and misdoings of our ancestors, none of us would be innocent and even be able to pay for damages. Several wars have been fought and territories conquered by mighty armies for reasons best known to them. Who knows, they might even be able to justify it as a means of survival, i.e. there was no other choice than to go to war or become extinct. It's in every human to desire survival. Greed couldn't have been the only reason some wars were fought; even love and other reasons one might not be able to think of could be reasons.

We have to let bygones be bygones and let go of the past. We can't control what has happened in the past, but we can influence what happens now and in the future. That notwithstanding, there is a place for justice because, without it, there can't be any meaningful and lasting peace. Settlement and retribution may need to be made to atone for past sins and offences against one another. According to a Yoruba adage, "We'll never have friends if we don't let go of past offences." The hate is so much between some tribes that families can disown one of their own who chooses to marry from that "abominable tribe." Some can even go to the extent of killing to prevent the marriage from consummating. A British lady once told me she was labelled as the black sheep of the family because she decided to marry a Nigerian man. She is just one of many outcasts present in the world because of their love lives. This is unfair, as people should be free to choose whoever they desire to be friends with, be in a relationship with, fall in love with and/or marry.

Another guy whose mom is British and whose dad is Nigerian once told me he struggled to fit in. He was always made to feel like he was not a whole family member whenever he was either with his Nigerian family or with the UK family. He narrated how his girlfriend (a Brit) felt terrible and feared for their unborn children when, on their way back from a night out, they were pulled over by the police, and what he described could only be "racial profiling." They eventually let them go after the typical line, "Sorry mate, we're only acting on instructions because your profile matches that of the suspect."

PROMOTING COMPASSION, EMPATHY, AND UNDERSTANDING AS TOOLS FOR CHANGE

Empathy is being able to walk (or imagine walking) in someone's shoes to understand where it hurts or how they're feeling fully. We should strive for understanding rather than tolerance. I think tolerating someone only brings about short-term results, while understanding them can help achieve long-lasting results. I once watched a Professor analyse the issue of migrants crossing into the UK at an alarming rate in a bid to seek asylum. I thought his solution was unarguably the most practical I've heard. He opined that you couldn't fathom why anyone would risk dying on a dangerous boat ride across the French-English channel to be in the UK as if once they get there, all their problems will disappear. They will become a brand new person entirely until you get to the root of why they left their home country in the first place. According to him, it's like a case of staying there and dying of starvation due to extreme poverty and poor infrastructure (electricity, portable water, affordable health care), amongst others or getting out to the land portrayed as heaven on earth. He summed it up by saying that some members of the UK parliament might do likewise if their existence were also threatened in their country. Historical data available on the internet confirms that there was a time when more people were emigrating than immigrating to the UK due to the harsh economic conditions back then. So, it's only natural for humans to seek survival by all means possible.

The point is we all want almost the same things as humans, and that is to survive or, better still, thrive. I'm sure that this must have been the motivating factor for the movement of people from one place to the other from time immemorial. Don't get me wrong, I'm totally against illegal immigration as it's criminal. It's not right for anyone to make themselves a burden and nuisance to many lawful and taxpaying citizens under the disguise of survival. It's okay to seek a better life (survive and, better still, thrive) as long as it's not to someone else's detriment.

A friend once described all kids as having a "territorial spirit." This was in reaction to watching his kids play with mine and argue and fight over my kids' toys. He called his son aside and asked him, "Do you also allow anyone to play with all your toys freely all the time?" He got the message that he's not in his territory, so he must calm down and play by the rules here. Like they say when in Rome, you have to behave like the Romans. What my friend was implying is that all kids have the tendency to be possessive, and it's up to parents to shape and guide them where necessary so it doesn't become excessive, leading to being too selfish, overly self-centred and narcissistic.

Adults are not left out of this behaviour. What can make an adult say to someone who appears to be from a different place, "Go back to your country?" In other words, the person is saying, "You're not welcome here any longer" or "You don't belong here", coming from a possessive and scarcity mindset. One of the principles I live by is that "we can all be successful without hurting one another because of the abundant resources in the world if only you can see it." The moment you feel that your current predicament is caused by someone else, even if you can't substantiate it, you'll likely be mean to them. The reason why some countries are hostile to foreigners is because they feel they've come to take their jobs. This reminds me of the Xenophobic attacks against Nigerians in South Africa a few years back, where it was in the news that some South African men were angry that their women were being taken by foreigners (with Nigeria as the prime target), so they have to find a way to exterminate them.

If only such men had the statistics to back their claim because, last time I checked, there are more women in the world than men. All you have to do is to have an open mind. I almost fell into that trap back in the days while in the corporate world in Nigeria, where some people felt threatened by Chinese, Americans, Europeans or foreigners generally because of the perception that they are on a mission to re-colonise them. One can be tempted to say they've got facts and reasons to be afraid, especially when those foreigners occupy the crème de la crème positions. Plus, there have been reported cases of inhumane treatment of Nigerian workers in some factories run by expatriates. This should not have anything to do with racial abuse; instead, the government should enforce employment laws.

FINAL THOUGHTS

A Vision for a United Future – #NoBlackNoWhiteJustHumans

"Ideologies separate us. Dreams and anguish bring us together."
– Eugene Ionesco

The Book's Central Message

The scourge of racism is an insidious cancer, eating away at the very fabric of our shared humanity. It leaves no corner of our global society untouched, inflicting untold suffering and hindering our collective progress. We have delved deep into the myriad ways racism and discrimination manifest, tearing at the seams of our communities, institutions, and interpersonal relationships.

Through the pages of this book, we have embarked on a journey of understanding. We have traced the historical roots of racism, examined its insidious characteristics, and explored the devastating impact it has on individuals, communities, and entire nations. We have confronted the uncomfortable truths of conscious and unconscious biases, those insidious whispers perpetuating inequality and injustice.

But this book is more than merely examining the problem; it is a call to action. It is a rallying cry to rise above the divisions that have plagued us for far too long. It is a plea to recognise that our true strength lies not in our differences but in our shared humanity.

Knowledge as a Catalyst for Change

I firmly believe that knowledge is the most potent weapon in our arsenal against racism and discrimination. By understanding the history, the psychology, and the societal structures that perpetuate these evils, we empower ourselves to dismantle them. We become agents of change, equipped with the tools to challenge discriminatory practices, to speak out against injustice, and to build a more equitable and inclusive world.

It is my sincere hope that this book will find its way onto the shelves of libraries, schools, universities, and corporate offices around the world. It will become a trusted resource for educators, policymakers, community leaders, and individuals seeking to expand their understanding of racism and its devastating consequences.

A Roadmap for Organisations

In today's interconnected world, organisations – particularly those with a global reach – have a unique responsibility to foster diversity, equality, and inclusion. This book serves as a roadmap for those organisations, offering practical guidance on how to identify and address discriminatory practices, create a more welcoming and equitable workplace, and cultivate a culture of respect and understanding.

By embracing the principles outlined in this book, organisations can unlock the full potential of their diverse workforce, enhance creativity and innovation, and build stronger, more resilient teams. They can become beacons of hope in a world too often marred by division and strife.

The Urgency of Now

We stand at a pivotal moment in human history. The forces of division and hatred are rearing their ugly heads, seeking to sow discord and undermine our progress toward a more just and equitable society. The time for complacency is over. The time for action is now.

We must each take personal responsibility for dismantling the systems of oppression that have held us back for far too long. We must educate ourselves and others about the insidious nature of racism and discrimination. We must challenge discriminatory practices wherever we encounter them. We must stand in solidarity with those who are marginalised and oppressed.

From Divided World to United World

Let us transform our divided world into a united one. Let us celebrate the rich tapestry of human diversity, recognising that our differences are not a source of weakness but strength. Let us create a world where every individual is valued, respected, and empowered to reach their full potential, regardless of their race, ethnicity, gender, sexual orientation, religion, or any other characteristic that makes them unique.

#NoBlackNoWhiteJustHumans

This is more than a hashtag; it is a philosophy, a way of life. It rejects the artificial constructs used to divide us for far too long. It is an affirmation of our shared humanity.

Let us embrace this philosophy with open hearts and open minds. Let us work tirelessly to create a world where the term "race" is associated solely with the "human race." Let us build a future where diversity is tolerated and celebrated as the spice of life.

In the words of the great Nelson Mandela, "No one is born hating another person because of the colour of his skin, background, or religion. People must learn to hate, and if they can learn to hate, they can be taught to love, for love comes more naturally to the human heart than its opposite."

Let us be the generation that teaches the world to love. Let us be the generation that finally breaks the chains of racism and discrimination. Let us be the generation that creates a united future for all humanity.

Enough is enough.

The time for change is now. Let us join hands, hearts, and minds to build a world where #NoBlackNoWhiteJustHumans is not just a slogan but a way of life.

ABOUT THE AUTHOR

Adetunji Banwo is an accomplished professional with a diverse background spanning over 15 years in project and program management, management consulting, coaching, mentoring, and professional speaking. He holds degrees from Lagos State Polytechnic, Ladoke Akintola University, and the University of Liverpool. Adetunji is a member of the Project Management Institute (PMI), USA, and the Nigerian Institute of Management (NIM).

In 2013, Adetunji founded Banwo Consulting Ltd in Nigeria, where he has personally trained over 5,000 individuals in project management. He also serves as the Lead Consultant at PROSHAP Ltd in the UK, focusing on developing cutting-edge learning solutions and providing consultancy and training services.

Currently residing in Ipswich, England, with his family, Adetunji's interests include learning, teaching, travelling, sports, and music. He is passionate about promoting diversity, equality, and inclusion in his professional and personal endeavours.

Adetunji Banwo has over 15 years of experience as a project and programs manager, management consultant, trainer, coach, mentor, and globally sought-after professional speaker. His alma mater includes Lagos State Polytechnic, Ladoke Akintola University, and the University of Liverpool. He is a member of the prestigious Project Management Institute (PMI), USA and the Nigerian Institute of Management (NIM).

Tunji, through the company he founded in 2013, Banwo Consulting Ltd [Nigeria], and working for various clients, have trained more than 5,000 persons on project management. He is also the Lead Consultant at PROSHAP Ltd [UK], where he champions the creation of various cutting-edge learning solutions whilst providing consultancy and training services.

He is based in Ipswich, England, with his family and enjoys learning, teaching, travelling, sports and music. He is very passionate about diversity, equality and inclusion.

REFERENCES

1. Achebe, C. (2012). *There Was a Country: A Personal History of Biafra*. Penguin Press.

2. Anthony, R. (2022). The challenge of ethnocentrism in Nigeria and the Ying-Yang principle of complementarity. *Aquino Journal of Philosophy, 2*(2).

3. Anti-Defamation League. (2019). Hate on Display™ Hate Symbols Database. Retrieved from https://www.adl.org/get-adls-hate-display-database-printable-resource

4. Anti-Defamation League. (n.d.). About Jewish people and the Holocaust. *ADL*. https://www.adl.org/about/mission-and-history

5. Azi, A. (2023). Apartheid policy in South Africa. *International Journal of Science and Society*. Retrieved from http://ijsoc.goacademica.com

6. BBC News. (n.d.). VV Brown – Racism & misogyny in the UK music industry. BBC News. https://www.bbc.co.uk/news/articles/cjk4nynd04po

7. Benjamin, B. (2017). Racism: Origin and theory. *Journal of Black Studies*. https://doi.org/10.1177/0021934717702135

8. Bizumic, B. (2015). Ethnocentrism. In R. A. Segal & K. von Stuckrad (Eds.), *Vocabulary for the study of religion* (Vol. 1). Leiden, the Netherlands: Brill Academic Publishers.

9. Bob, K. The impact of slavery on modern Africa. Retrieved from https://www.fairplanet.org/dossier/beyond-slavery/the-impact-of-slavery-on-modern-africa/

10. Braveman, P. A., Arkin, E., Proctor, D., Kauh, T., & Holm, N. (2022). Systemic and structural racism: Definitions, examples, health damages, and approaches to dismantling. *Health Affairs (Millwood)*, *41*(2), 171-178. https://doi.org/10.1377/hlthaff.2021.01394

11. Castle, S. (1993). Racism: A global analysis. *Centre for Multicultural Studies, University of Wollongong*. Occasional Paper 28, 45. Retrieved from https://ro.edu.au/cmsocpapers/26

12. Cogburn, C. (2024). The impact of racism on Black American mental health. *National Library of Medicine*.

13. Collete, A. (2015). The residuals of colonial rule and its impact on the process of racialisation in Uganda. *CERS*

Working Paper.

14. Dodd, V. (2024, January 5). Head of Britain's police chiefs says force 'institutionally racist'. *The Guardian.* Retrieved from https://www.theguardian.com/uk-news/2024/jan/05/head-of-britains-police-chiefs-says-force-institutionally-racist

15. Edward, M. (2021). Racial alienation in Africa: A post-colonial reading of Doris Lessing's No witchcraft for sale. *Journal of Public Affairs.* Retrieved from https://www.researchgate.net/publication/254465610

16. Equal Justice Initiative. The transatlantic slave trade. Retrieved from https://eji.org/report/transatlantic-slave-trade/

17. Ethnicity facts and figures. (n.d.). Writing about ethnicity. *UK Government.* https://www.ethnicity-facts-figures.service.gov.uk/style-guide/writing-about-ethnicity/

18. Gross, R. (2020). The psychology of prejudice. *ResearchGate.* https://doi.org/10.4324/9781003082040

19. Grosfoguel, R. (2016). What is racism? *World-Systems Research.* https://doi.org/10.5195/jwsr.2016.609

20. Independent. (2023, September 26). Gymnastics Ireland racism medal video. *Independent.* https://www.independent.co.uk/tv/news/gymnastics-ireland-racism-medal-

video-b2417926.html

21. John, F. D., Miles, H., Peter, G., & Victoria, M. E. Prejudice, stereotyping and discrimination: Theoretical and empirical overview.

22. Jonelle, A. Culture matters: Managing unconscious bias.

23. Law Insider. Individual racism. Retrieved from https://www.lawinsider.com/dictionary/individual-racism

24. Manya, S. (2016). U.S. mass media portrayal of the African continent: The African perspective. *West Texas A & M University, Canyon, Texas.*

25. Melanie, D., et al. (2022). Addressing the interlocking impact of colonialism and racism on Filipinx/a/o American health inequities. *Health Affairs, 41*(2), 289-295. https://doi.org/10.1377/hlthaff.2021.01418

26. Nunn, N. (2010). The long-term effects of Africa's slave trades. *Quarterly Journal of Economics, 123,* 139-176.

27. Peterson, C. (2024). The countries where Christianity is illegal in 2024. *Persecution Trends to Watch.*

28. Punch Newspapers. (2024). Plateau killings: Burning churches, mosques, barbaric, says MURIC.

29. Ramon, G. (2016). What is racism? *University Library System.* University of Pittsburgh Press.

30. Richard, L. (2017). Cognitive bias: Recognising and managing our unconscious bias. *The Pharos.*

31. Richard, S. (2023). Racism takes a toll on the brain, research shows. *The Washington Post.*

32. Steven, R. (2020). Stanford psychologist identifies seven factors that contribute to American racism. *Stanford Report.*

33. Sebastiaan, V. (2020). Racism amongst white Afrikaner adolescents: The challenge of I-Thou (Buber) relations. *HTS Teologiese Studies/Theological Studies, 76*(2), a5240. https://doi.org/10.4102/hts.v76i2.5240

34. The Editors of Encyclopaedia Britannica. Transatlantic slave trade key facts. Retrieved from https://www.britannica.com/summary/Transatlantic-Slave-Trade-Key-Facts

35. The Guardian. (2023, March 14). Eleanor Williams jailed for lying about rapes and trafficking. *The Guardian.* https://www.theguardian.com/uk-news/2023/mar/14/eleanor-williams-jailed-lying-rapes-trafficking

36. The Guardian. (2024, March 22). Kemi Badenoch on EDI. *The Guardian.* https://www.theguardian.com/commentisfree/2024/mar/22/kemi-badenoch-diversity-schemes-career-equalities-minister-tory

37. The Guardian. (2024). Institutional racism in UK police. Retrieved from https://www.theguardian.com/uk-news/2024/jan/05/head-of-britains-police-chiefs-says-force-is-institutionally-racist-gavin-stephens

38. The New York Times. (2020, May 31). George Floyd case. The New York Times. https://www.nytimes.com/2020/05/31/us/george-floyd-investigation.html

39. United Nations Human Rights. Office of the High Commissioner. Racism, discrimination are legacies of colonialism. Retrieved from https://www.ohchr.org/en/get-involved/stories/racism-discrimination-are-legacies-colonialism

40. White, A. (2020). *Leadership Philosophy*. Retrieved from http://maase.pbworks.com/w/file/fetch/140375337/AdamWhite_6.2.20_Session2_Ldrsp%20Philosophy.pdf

TUNJI BANWO